ISBN 978-1-330-01266-6
PIBN 10003791

When the Courts of the State of New York upheld the fraudulent methods by which I was disfranchised and my American citizenship of thirty-two years denied me, I waived my right of appeal in order that I might return to Russia and help in the great work. I believed fervently that the Bolsheviki were furthering the Revolution and exerting themselves in behalf of the people. I clung to my faith and belief for more than a year after my coming to Russia.

Observation and study, extensive travel through various parts of the country, meeting with every shade of political opinion and every variety of friend and enemy of the Bolsheviki— all convinced me of the ghastly delusion which had been foisted upon the world.

I refer to these circumstances to indicate that my change of mind and heart was a painful and difficult process, and that my final decision to speak out is for the sole reason that the people everywhere may learn to differentiate between the Bolsheviki and the Russian Revolution.

The conventional conception of gratitude is that one must not be critical of those who have shown him kindness. Thanks to this notion parents enslave their children more effectively than by brutal treatment; and by it friends tyrannize over one another. In fact, all human relationships are to-day vitiated by this noxious idea.

Some people have upbraided me for my critical attitude toward the Bolsheviki. "How ungrateful to attack the Communist Government after the hospitality and kindness she enjoyed in Russia," they indignantly exclaim. I do not mean to gainsay that I have received advantages while I was in Russia. I could have received many more had I been willing to serve the powers that be. It is that very circumstance which has made it bitter hard for me to speak out against the evils as I saw them day by day. But finally I realized that silence is indeed a sign of consent.

Not to cry out against the betrayal of the Russian Revolution would have made me a party to that betrayal. The Revolution and the welfare of the masses in and out of Russia are by far too important to me to allow any personal consideration for the Communists I have met and learned to respect to obscure my sense of justice and to cause me to refrain from giving to the world my two years' experience in Russia.

In certain quarters objections will no doubt be raised because I have given no names of the persons I am quoting. Some may even exploit the fact to discredit my veracity. But I prefer to face that rather than to turn any one over to the tender mercies of the Tcheka, which would inevitably result were I to divulge the names of the Communists or non-Communists who felt free to speak to me. Those familiar with the real situation in Russia and who are not under the mesmeric influence of the Bolshevik superstition or in the employ of the Communists will bear me out that I have given a true picture. The rest of the world will learn in due time.

Friends whose opinion I value have been good enough to suggest that my quarrel with the Bolsheviki is due to my social philosophy rather than to the failure of the Bolshevik régime. As

an Anarchist, they claim, I would naturally in-
sist on the importance of the individual and of
personal liberty, but in the revolutionary period
both must be subordinated to the good of the
whole. Other friends point out that destruction,
violence, and terrorism are inevitable factors in
a revolution. As a revolutionist, they say, I
cannot consistently object to the violence practised by the Bolsheviki.

Both these criticisms would be justified had I
come to Russia expecting to find Anarchism realized, or if I were to maintain that revolutions can
be made peacefully. Anarchism to me never
was a mechanistic arrangement of social relationships to be imposed upon man by political
scene-shifting or by a transfer of power from one
social class to another. Anarchism to me was
and is the child, not of destruction, but of con-
struction—the result of growth and development of the conscious creative social efforts of a
regenerated people. I do not therefore expect
Anarchism to follow in the immediate footsteps
of centuries of despotism and submission. And
I certainly did not expect to see it ushered in
by the Marxian theory.

I did, however, hope to find in Russia at least
the beginnings of the social changes for which

the Revolution had been fought. Not the fate of the individual was my main concern as a revolutionist. I should have been content if the Russian workers and peasants as a whole had derived essential social betterment as a result of the Bolshevik régime.

Two years of earnest study, investigation, and research convinced me that the great benefits brought to the Russian people by Bolshevism exist only on paper, painted in glowing colours to the masses of Europe and America by efficient Bolshevik propaganda. As advertising wizards the Bolsheviki excel anything the world had ever known before. But in reality the Russian people have gained nothing from the Bolshevik experiment. To be sure, the peasants have the land; not by the grace of the Bolsheviki, but through their own direct efforts, set in motion long before the October change. That the peasants were able to retain the land is due mostly to the static Slav tenacity; owing to the circumstance that they form by far the largest part of the population and are deeply rooted in the soil, they could not as easily be torn away from it as the workers from their means of production.

The Russian workers, like the peasants, also

employed direct action. They possessed themselves of the factories, organized their own shop committees, and were virtually in control of the economic life of Russia. But soon they were stripped of their power and placed under the industrial yoke of the Bolshevik State. Chattel slavery became the lot of the Russian proletariat. It was suppressed and exploited in the name of something which was later to bring it comfort, light, and warmth. Try as I might I could find nowhere any evidence of benefits received either by the workers or the peasants from the Bolshevik régime.

On the other hand, I did find the revolutionary faith of the people broken, the spirit of solidarity crushed, the meaning of comradeship and mutual helpfulness distorted. One must have lived in Russia, close to the everyday affairs of the people; one must have seen and felt their utter disillusionment and despair to appreciate fully the disintegrating effect of the Bolshevik principle and methods—disintegrating all that was once the pride and the glory of revolutionary Russia.

The argument that destruction and terror are part of revolution I do not dispute. I know that in the past every great political and social change necessitated violence. America might still be under the British yoke but for the heroic colonists who dared to oppose British tyranny by force of arms. Black slavery might still be a legalized institution in the United States but for the militant spirit of the John Browns. I have never denied that violence is inevitable, nor do I gainsay it now. Yet it is one thing to employ violence in combat, as a means of defence. [It is quite another thing to make a principle of terrorism, to institutionalize it, to assign it the most vital place in the social struggle. Such terrorism begets counter-revolution and in turn itself becomes counter-revolutionary.

Rarely has a revolution been fought with as little violence as the Russian Revolution. Nor would have Red Terror followed had the people and the cultural forces remained in control of the Revolution. This was demonstrated by the spirit of fellowship and solidarity which prevailed throughout Russia during the first months after the October revolution. But an insignificant minority bent on creating an absolute State is necessarily driven to oppression and terrorism.

There is another objection to my criticism on the part of the Communists. Russia is on strike, they say, and it is unethical for a revolutionist to side against the workers when they are striking against their masters. That is pure demagoguery practised by the Bolsheviki to silence criticism.

It is not true that the Russian people are on strike. On the contrary, the truth of the matter is that the Russian people have been *locked out* and that the Bolshevik State—even as the bourgeois industrial master—uses the sword and the gun to keep the people out. In the case of the Bolsheviki this tyranny is masked by a world-stirring slogan: thus they have succeeded in blinding the masses. Just because I am a revolutionist I refuse to side with the master class, which in Russia is called the Communist Party.

Till the end of my days my place shall be with the disinherited and oppressed. It is immaterial to me whether Tyranny rules in the Kremlin or in any other seat of the mighty. I could do nothing for suffering Russia while in that country. Perhaps I can do something now by pointing out the lessons of the Russian experience. Not my concern for the Russian people only has prompted the writing of this volume: it is my interest in the masses everywhere.

The masses, like the individual, may not

readily learn from the experience of others. Yet those who have gained the experience must speak out, if for no other reason than that they cannot in justice to themselves and their ideal support the great delusion revealed to them.

EMMA GOLDMAN.

Berlin, July, 1922.

MY DISILLUSIONMENT
IN RUSSIA

MY DISILLUSIONMENT IN RUSSIA

CHAPTER I

DEPORTATION TO RUSSIA

ON THE night of December 21, 1919, together with two hundred and forty-eight other political prisoners, I was deported from America. Although it was generally known we were to be deported, few really believed that the United States would so completely deny her past as an asylum for political refugees, some of whom had lived and worked in America for more than thirty years.

In my own case, the decision to eliminate me first became known when, in 1909, the Federal authorities went out of their way to disfranchise the man whose name gave me citizenship. That Washington waited till 1917 was due to the circumstance that the psychologic moment for the finale was lacking. Perhaps I should have contested my case at that time. With the then-prevalent public opinion, the Courts would probably not have sustained the fraudulent proceedings which robbed me of citizenship. But it did not seem credible then that America would stoop to the Tsaristic method of deportation.

Our anti-war agitation added fuel to the war hysteria of 1917, and thus furnished the Federal authorities with the desired opportunity to complete the conspiracy begun against me in Rochester, N. Y., 1909.

It was on December 5, 1919, while in Chicago lecturing, that I was telegraphically apprised of the fact that the order for my deportation was final. The question of my citizenship was then raised in court, but was of course decided adversely. I had intended to take the case to a higher tribunal, but finally I decided to carry the matter no further: Soviet Russia was luring me.

Ludicrously secretive were the authorities about our deportation. To the very last moment we were kept in ignorance as to the time. Then, unexpectedly, in the wee small hours of December 21st we were spirited away. The scene set for this performance was most thrilling. It was six o'clock Sunday morning, December

21, 1919, when under heavy military convoy we stepped aboard the *Buford*.

For twenty-eight days we were prisoners. Sentries at our cabin doors day and night, sentries on deck during the hour we were daily permitted to breathe the fresh air. Our men comrades were cooped up in dark, damp quarters, wretchedly fed, all of us in complete ignorance of the direction we were to take. Yet our spirits were high—Russia, free, new Russia was before us.

All my life Russia's heroic struggle for freedom was as a beacon to me. The revolutionary zeal of her martyred men and women, which neither fortress nor *katorga* could suppress, was my inspiration in the darkest hours. When the news of the February Revolution flashed across the world, I longed to hasten to the land which had performed the miracle and had freed her people from the age-old yoke of Tsarism. But America held me. The thought of thirty years of struggle for my ideals, of my friends and associates, made it impossible to tear myself away. I would go to Russia later, I thought.

Then came America's entry into the war and the need of remaining true to the American people who were swept into the hurricane against

their will.   After all, I owed a great debt, I owed
my growth and development to what was finest
and best in America, to her fighters for liberty,
[to the sons and daughters of the revolution to
come.] I would be true to them.   But the
frenzied militarists soon terminated my work.

At last I was bound for Russia and all else was
almost blotted out.   I would behold with mine
own eyes *matushka Rossiya*, the land freed from
political and economic masters; the Russian
dubinushka, as the peasant was called, raised
from the dust; the Russian worker, the modern
Samson, who with a sweep of his mighty arm had
pulled down the pillars of decaying society.   The
twenty-eight days on our floating prison passed
in a sort of trance.   I was hardly conscious of
my surroundings.

Finally we reached Finland, across which we
were forced to journey in sealed cars.   On the
Russian border we were met by a committee of
the Soviet Government, headed by Zorin.   They
had come to greet the first political refugees
[driven from America for opinion's sake.]

It was a cold day, with the earth a sheet of
white, but spring was in our hearts.   Soon we
were to behold revolutionary Russia.   I preferred to be alone when I touched the sacred

soil: my exaltation was too great, and I feared I might not be able to control my emotion. When I reached Beloöstrov the first enthusiastic reception tendered the refugees was over, but the place was still surcharged with intensity of feeling. I could sense the awe and humility of our group who, treated like felons in the United States, were here received as dear brothers and comrades and welcomed by the Red soldiers, the liberators of Russia.

From Beloöstrov we were driven to the village where another reception had been prepared: A dark hall filled to suffocation, the platform lit up by tallow candles, a huge red flag, on the stage a group of women in black nuns' attire. I stood as in a dream in the breathless silence. Suddenly a voice rang out. It beat like metal on my ears and seemed uninspired, but it spoke of the great suffering of the Russian people and of the enemies of the Revolution. Others addressed the audience, but I was held by the women in black, their faces ghastly in the yellow light. Were these really nuns? Had the Revolution penetrated even the walls of superstition? Had the Red Dawn broken into the narrow lives of these ascetics? It all seemed strange, fascinating.

Somehow I found myself on the platform. I could only blurt out that like my comrades I had not come to Russia to teach: I had come to learn, to draw sustenance and hope from her, to lay down my life on the altar of the Revolution.

After the meeting we were escorted to the waiting Petrograd train, the women in the black hood intoning the "Internationale," the whole audience joining in. I was in the car with our host, Zorin, who had lived in America and spoke English fluently. He talked enthusiastically about the Soviet Government and its marvellous achievements. His conversation was illuminative, but one phrase struck me as discordant. Speaking of the political organization of his Party, he remarked: "Tammany Hall has nothing on us, and as to Boss Murphy, we could teach him a thing or two." I thought the man was jesting. What relation could there be between Tammany Hall, Boss Murphy, and the Soviet Government?

I inquired about our comrades who had hastened from America at the first news of the Revolution. Many of them had died at the front, Zorin informed me, others were working with the Soviet Government. And Shatov? William Shatov, a brilliant speaker and able organizer, was a well-known figure in America, frequently associated with us in our work. We had sent him a telegram from Finland and were much surprised at his failure to reply. Why did not Shatov come to meet us? "Shatov had to leave for Siberia, where he is to take the post of Minister of Railways," said Zorin.

In Petrograd our group again received an ovation. Then the deportees were taken to the famous Tauride Palace, where they were to be fed and housed for the night. Zorin asked Alexander Berkman and myself to accept his hospitality. We entered the waiting automobile. The city was dark and deserted; not a living soul to be seen anywhere. We had not gone very far when the car was suddenly halted, and an electric light flashed into our eyes. It was the militia, demanding the password. (Petrograd had recently fought back the Yudenitch attack and was still under martial law. The process was repeated frequently along the route. Shortly before we reached our destination we passed a well-lighted building "It is our station house," Zorin explained, "but we have few prisoners there now. Capital punishment is abolished and we have recently proclaimed a general political amnesty."

Presently the automobile came to a halt.
"The First House of the Soviets," said Zorin,
"the living place of the most active members of
our Party." Zorin and his wife occupied two
rooms, simply but comfortably furnished. Tea
and refreshments were served, and our hosts
entertained us with the absorbing story of the
marvellous defence the Petrograd workers had
organized against the Yudenitch forces. How
heroically the men and women, even the children, had rushed to the defence of the Red City!
What wonderful self-discipline and coöperation the proletariat demonstrated. The evening
passed in these reminiscences, and I was about to
retire to the room secured for me when a young
woman arrived who introduced herself as the
sister-in-law of "Bill" Shatov. She greeted us
warmly and asked us to come up to see her sister
who lived on the floor above. When we reached
their apartment I found myself embraced by
big jovial Bill himself. How strange of Zorin to
tell me that Shatov had left for Siberia! What
did it mean? Shatov explained that he had
been ordered not to meet us at the border, to
prevent his giving us our first impressions of
Soviet Russia. He had fallen into disfavour
with the Government and was being sent to

Siberia into virtual exile. His trip had been delayed and therefore we still happened to find him.

We spent much time with Shatov before he left Petrograd. For whole days I listened to his story of the Revolution, with its light and shadows, and the developing tendency of the Bolsheviki toward the right. Shatov, however, insisted that it was necessary for all the revolutionary elements to work with the Bolsheviki Government. Of course, the Communists had made many mistakes, but what they did was inevitable, imposed upon them by Allied interference and the blockade.

A few days after our arrival Zorin asked Alexander Berkman and myself to accompany him to Smolny. Smolny, the erstwhile boarding school for the daughters of the aristocracy, had been the centre of revolutionary events. Almost every stone had played its part. Now it was the seat of the Petrograd Government. I found the place heavily guarded and giving the impression of a beehive of officials and government employees. The Department of the Third International was particularly interesting. It was the domain of Zinoviev. I was much impressed by the magnitude of it all.

After showing us about, Zorin invited us to the Smolny dining room. The meal consisted of good soup, meat and potatoes, bread and tea—rather a good meal in starving Russia, I thought.

Our group of deportees was quartered in Smolny. I was anxious about my travelling companions, the two girls who had shared my cabin on the *Buford*. I wished to take them back with me to the First House of the Soviet. Zorin sent for them. They arrived greatly excited and told us that the whole group of deportees had been placed under military guard. The news was startling. The people who had been driven out of America for their political opinions, now in Revolutionary Russia again prisoners—three days after their arrival. What had happened?

We turned to Zorin. He seemed embarrassed. "Some mistake," he said, and immediately began to make inquiries. It developed that four ordinary criminals had been found among the politicals deported by the United States Government, and therefore a guard was placed over the whole group. The proceeding seemed to me unjust and uncalled for. It was my first lesson in Bolshevik methods.

CHAPTER II

PETROGRAD

MY PARENTS had moved to St. Petersburg when I was thirteen. Under the discipline of a German school in Königsberg and the Prussian attitude toward everything Russian, I had grown up in the atmosphere of hatred to that country. I dreaded especially the terrible Nihilists who had killed Tsar Alexander II, so good and kind, as I had been taught. St. Petersburg was to me an evil thing. But the gayety of the city, its vivacity and brilliancy, soon dispelled my childish fancies and made the city appear like a fairy dream. Then my curiosity was aroused by the revolutionary mystery which seemed to hang over everyone, and of which no one dared to speak. When four years later I left with my sister for America I was no longer the German Gretchen to whom Russia spelt evil. My whole soul had been transformed and the seed planted for what was to be my life's work. Especially did St. Petersburg remain in my memory a vivid picture, full of life and mystery.

I found Petrograd of 1920 quite a different place. It was almost in ruins, as if a hurricane had swept over it. The houses looked like broken old tombs upon neglected and forgotten cemeteries. The streets were dirty and deserted; all life had gone from them. The population of Petrograd before the war was almost two million; in 1920 it had dwindled to five hundred thousand. The people walked about like living corpses; the shortage of food and fuel was slowly sapping the city; grim death was clutching at its heart. Emaciated and frost-bitten men, women, and children were being whipped by the common lash, the search for a piece of bread or a stick of wood. It was a heart-rending sight by day, an oppressive weight at night. Especially were the nights of the first month in Petrograd dreadful. The utter stillness of the large city was paralysing. It fairly haunted me, this awful oppressive silence broken only by occasional shots. I would lay awake trying to pierce the mystery. Did not Zorin say that capital punishment had been abolished? Why this shooting? Doubts disturbed my mind, but I tried to wave them aside. I had come to learn.

Much of my first knowledge and impressions of the October Revolution and the events that followed I received from the Zorins. As already mentioned, both had lived in America, spoke English, and were eager to enlighten me upon the history of the Revolution. They were devoted to the cause and worked very hard; he, especially, who was secretary of the Petrograd committee of his party, besides editing the daily, *Krasnaya Gazetta*, and participating in other activities.

It was from Zorin that I first learned about that legendary figure, Makhno. The latter was an Anarchist, I was informed, who under the Tsar had been sentenced to *katorga*. Liberated by the February revolution, he became the leader of a peasant army in the Ukraina, proving himself extremely able and daring and doing splendid work in the defence of the Revolution. For some time Makhno worked in harmony with the Bolsheviki, fighting the counter-revolutionary forces. Then he became antagonistic, and now his army, recruited from bandit elements, was fighting the Bolsheviki. Zorin related that he had been one of a committee sent to Makhno to bring about an understanding. But Makhno would not listen to reason. He continued his warfare against the Soviets and was considered a dangerous counter-revolutionist.

I had no means of verifying the story, and I was far from disbelieving the Zorins. Both appeared most sincere and dedicated to their work, types of religious zealots ready to burn the heretic, but equally ready to sacrifice their own lives for their cause. I was much impressed by the simplicity of their lives. Holding a responsible position, Zorin could have received special rations, but they lived very poorly, their supper often consisting only of herring, black bread, and tea. I thought it especially admirable because Lisa Zorin was with child at the time.

Two weeks after my arrival in Russia I was invited to attend the Alexander Herzen commemoration in the Winter Palace. The white marble hall where the gathering took place seemed to intensify the bitter frost, but the people present were unmindful of the penetrating cold. I also was conscious only of the unique situation: Alexander Herzen, one of the most hated revolutionists of his time, honoured in the Winter Palace! Frequently before the spirit of Herzen had found its way into the house of the Romanovs. It was when the "Kolokol," published abroad and sparkling with the brilliancy of

Herzen and Turgenev, would in some mysterious manner be discovered on the desk of the Tsar. Now the Tsars were no more, but the spirit of Herzen had risen again and was witnessing the realization of the dream of one of Russia's great men.

One evening I was informed that Zinoviev had returned from Moscow and would see me. He arrived about midnight. He looked very tired and was constantly disturbed by urgent messages. Our talk was of a general nature, of the grave situation in Russia, the shortage of food and fuel then particularly poignant, and about the labour situation in America. He was anxious to know "how soon the revolution could be expected in the United States." He left upon me no definite impression, but I was conscious of something lacking in the man, though I could not determine at the time just what it was.

Another Communist I saw much of the first weeks was John Reed. I had known him in America. He was living in the Astoria, working hard and preparing for his return to the United States. He was to journey through Latvia and he seemed apprehensive of the outcome. He had been in Russia during the October days and this was his second visit. Like Shatov he also insisted that the dark sides of the Bolshevik régime were inevitable. He believed fervently that the Soviet Government would emerge from its narrow party lines and that it would presently establish the Communistic Commonwealth. We spent much time together, discussing the various phases of the situation.

So far I had met none of the Anarchists and their failure to call rather surprised me. One day a friend I had known in the States came to inquire whether I would see several members of an Anarchist organization. I readily assented. From them I learned a version of the Russian Revolution and the Bolshevik régime utterly different from what I had heard before. It was so startling, so terrible that I could not believe it. They invited me to attend a small gathering they had called to present to me their views.

The following Sunday I went to their conference. Passing Nevsky Prospekt, near Liteiny Street, I came upon a group of women huddled together to protect themselves from the cold. They were surrounded by soldiers, talking and gesticulating. Those women, I learned, were prostitutes who were selling themselves for a pound of bread, a piece of soap or chocolate. The soldiers were the only ones who could af-

ford to buy them because of their extra rations.
Prostitution in revolutionary Russia. I wondered. What is the Communist Government
doing for these unfortunates? What are the
Workers' and Peasants' Soviets doing? My
escort smiled sadly. The Soviet Government
had closed the houses of prostitution and was
now trying to drive the women off the streets, but
hunger and cold drove them back again; besides,
the soldiers had to be humoured. It was too
ghastly, too incredible to be real, yet there they
were—those shivering creatures for sale and their
buyers, the red defenders of the Revolution.
"The cursed interventionists, the blockade—
they are responsible," said my escort. Why,
yes, the counter-revolutionists and the blockade
are responsible, I reassured myself. I tried to
dismiss the thought of that huddled group, but
it clung to me. I felt something snap within me.

At last we reached the Anarchist quarters, in
a dilapidated house in a filthy backyard. I was
ushered into a small room crowded with men and
women. The sight recalled pictures of thirty
years ago when, persecuted and hunted from
place to place, the Anarchists in America were
compelled to meet in a dingy hall on Orchard
Street, New York, or in the dark rear room of a

saloon. That was in capitalistic America. But this is revolutionary Russia, which the Anarchists had helped to free. Why should they have to gather in secret and in such a place?

That evening and the following day I listened to a recital of the betrayal of the Revolution by the Bolsheviki. Workers from the Baltic factories spoke of their enslavement, Kronstadt sailors voiced their bitterness and indignation against the people they had helped to power and who had become their masters. One of the speakers had been condemned to death by the Bolsheviki for his Anarchist ideas, but had escaped and was now living illegally. He related how the sailors had been robbed of the freedom of their Soviets, how every breath of life was being censored. Others spoke of the Red Terror and repression in Moscow, which resulted in the throwing of a bomb into the gathering of the Moscow section of the Communist Party in September, 1919. They told me of the over-filled prisons, of the violence practised on the workers and peasants. I listened rather impatiently, for everything in me cried out against this indictment. It sounded impossible; it could not be. Someone was surely at fault, but probably it was they, my comrades, I thought. They were unreasonable, impatient for immediate results. Was not violence inevitable in a revolution, and was it not imposed upon the Bolsheviki by the Interventionists? My comrades were indignant. "Disguise yourself so the Bolsheviki do not recognize you; take a pamphlet of Kropotkin and try to distribute it in a Soviet meeting. You will soon see whether we told you the truth. Above all, get out of the First House of the Soviet. Live among the people and you will have all the proofs you need."

How childish and trifling it all seemed in the face of the world event that was taking place in Russia! No, I could not credit their stories. I would wait and study conditions. But my mind was in a turmoil, and the nights became more oppressive than ever.

The day arrived when I was given a chance to attend the meeting of the Petro-Soviet. It was to be a double celebration in honour of the return of Karl Radek to Russia and Joffe's report on the peace treaty with Esthonia. As usual I went with the Zorins. The gathering was in the Tauride Palace, the former meeting place of the Russian Duma. Every entrance to the hall was guarded by soldiers, the platform surrounded by them holding their guns at attention.

The hall was crowded to the very doors. I was on the platform overlooking the sea of faces below. Starved and wretched they looked, these sons and daughters of the people, the heroes of Red Petrograd. How they had suffered and endured for the Revolution! I felt very humble before them.

Zinoviev presided. After the "Internationale" had been sung by the audience standing, Zinoviev opened the meeting. He spoke at length. His voice is high pitched, without depth. The moment I heard him I realized what I had missed in him at our first meeting—depth, strength of character. Next came Radek. He was clever, witty, sarcastic, and he paid his respects to the counter-revolutionists and to the White Guards. Altogether an interesting man and an interesting address.

Joffe looked the diplomat. Well fed and groomed, he seemed rather out of place in that assembly. He spoke of the peace conditions with Esthonia, which were received with enthusiasm by the audience. Certainly these people wanted peace. Would it ever come to Russia?

Last spoke Zorin, by far the ablest and most convincing that evening. Then the meeting was thrown open to discussion. A Menshevik asked for the floor. Immediately pandemonium broke loose. Yells of "Traitor!" "Kolchak!" "Counter-Revolutionist!" came from all parts of the audience and even from the platform. It looked to me like an unworthy proceeding for a revolutionary assembly.

On the way home I spoke to Zorin about it. He laughed. "Free speech is a bourgeois superstition," he said; "during a revolutionary period there can be no free speech." I was rather dubious about the sweeping statement, but I felt that I had no right to judge. I was a newcomer, while the people at the Tauride Palace had sacrificed and suffered so much for the Revolution. I had no right to judge.

CHAPTER III

DISTURBING THOUGHTS

LIFE went on. Each day brought new conflicting thoughts and emotions. The feature which affected me most was the inequality I witnessed in my immediate environment. I learned that the rations issued to the tenants of the First House of the Soviet (Astoria) were much superior to those received by the workers in the factories. To be sure, they were not sufficient to sustain life—but no one in the Astoria lived from these rations alone. The members of the Communist Party, quartered in the Astoria, worked in Smolny, and the rations in Smolny were the best in Petrograd. Moreover, trade was not entirely suppressed at that time. The markets were doing a lucrative business, though no one seemed able or willing to explain to me where the purchasing capacity came from. The workers could not afford to buy butter which was then 2,000 rubles a pound, sugar at 3,000, or meat at 1,000. The inequality was most apparent in the Astoria kitchen. I went there frequently, though it was torture to prepare a meal: the savage scramble for an inch of space on the stove, the greedy watching of the women lest any one have something extra in the saucepan, the quarrels and screams when someone fished out a piece of meat from the pot of a neighbour! But there was one redeeming feature in the picture—it was the resentment of the servants who worked in the Astoria. They were servants, though called comrades, and they felt keenly the inequality: the Revolution to them was not a mere theory to be realized in years to come. It was a living thing. I was made aware of it one day.

The rations were distributed at the Commissary, but one had to fetch them himself. One day, while waiting my turn in the long line, a peasant girl came in and asked for vinegar. "Vinegar! who is it calls for such a luxury?" cried several women. It appeared that the girl was Zinoviev's servant. She spoke of him as her master, who worked very hard and was surely entitled to something extra. At once a storm of indignation broke loose. "Master! is that what we made the Revolution for, or was it to do away with masters? Zinoviev is no more than we, and he is not entitled to more."

These workingwomen were crude, even brutal, but their sense of justice was instinctive. The Revolution to them was something fundamentally vital. They saw the inequality at every step and bitterly resented it. I was disturbed. I sought to reassure myself that Zinoviev and the other leaders of the Communists would not use their power for selfish benefit. It was the shortage of food and the lack of efficient organization which made it impossible to feed all alike, and of course the blockade and not the Bolsheviki was responsible for it. The Allied Interventionists, who were trying to get at Russia's throat, were the cause.

Every Communist I met reiterated this thought; even some of the Anarchists insisted on it. The little group antagonistic to the Soviet Government was not convincing. But how reconcile the explanation given to me with some of the stories I learned every day—stories of systematic terrorism, of relentless persecution, and suppression of other revolutionary elements?

Another circumstance which perplexed me was that the markets were stacked with meat, fish, soap, potatoes, even shoes, every time that the rations were given out. How did these things get to the markets? Everyone spoke about it, but no one seemed to know. One day I was in a watchmaker's shop when a soldier entered. He conversed with the proprietor in Yiddish, relating that he had just returned from Siberia with a shipment of tea. Would the watchmaker take fifty pounds? Tea was sold at a premium at the time—no one but the privileged few could permit themselves such a luxury. Of course the watchmaker would take the tea. When the soldier left I asked the shopkeeper if he did not think it rather risky to transact such illegal business so openly. I happen to understand Yiddish, I told him. Did he not fear I would report him? "That's nothing," the man replied nonchalantly, "the Tcheka knows all about it—it draws its percentage from the soldier and myself."

I began to suspect that the reason for much of the evil was also within Russia, not only outside of it. But then, I argued, police officials and detectives graft everywhere. That is the common disease of the breed. In Russia, where scarcity of food and three years of starvation must needs turn most people into grafters, theft is inevitable. The Bolsheviki are trying to suppress it with an iron hand. How can they be blamed? But try as I might I could not silence my doubts. I groped for some moral support, for a dependable word, for someone to shed light on the disturbing questions.

It occurred to me to write to Maxim Gorki. He might help. I called his attention to his own dismay and disappointment while visiting America. He had come believing in her democracy and liberalism, and found bigotry and lack of hospitality instead. I felt sure Gorki would understand the struggle going on within me, though the cause was not the same. Would he see me? Two days later I received a short note asking me to call.

I had admired Gorki for many years. He was the living affirmation of my belief that the creative artist cannot be suppressed. Gorki, the child of the people, the pariah, had by his genius become one of the world's greatest, one who by his pen and deep human sympathy made the social outcast our kin. For years I toured America interpreting Gorki's genius to the American people, elucidating the greatness, beauty, and humanity of the man and his works. Now I was to see him and through him get a glimpse into the complex soul of Russia.

I found the main entrance of his house nailed up, and there seemed to be no way of getting in. I almost gave up in despair when a woman pointed to a dingy staircase. I climbed to the very top and knocked on the first door I saw. It was thrown open, momentarily blinding me with a flood of light and steam from an overheated kitchen. Then I was ushered into a large dining room. It was dimly lit, chilly and cheerless in spite of a fire and a large collection of Dutch china on the walls. One of the three women I had noticed in the kitchen sat down at the table with me, pretending to read a book but all the while watching me out of the corner of her eye. It was an awkward half hour of waiting.

Presently Gorki arrived. Tall, gaunt, and coughing, he looked ill and weary. He took me to his study, semi-dark and of depressing effect. No sooner had we seated ourselves than the door flew open and another young woman, whom I had not observed before, brought him a glass of dark fluid, medicine evidently. Then the telephone began to ring; a few minutes later Gorki was called out of the room. I realized that I would not be able to talk with him. Returning, he must have noticed my disappointment. We agreed to postpone our talk till some less disturbed opportunity presented itself. He escorted me to the door, remarking, "You ought to visit the Baltflot [Baltic Fleet]. The Kronstadt sailors are nearly all instinctive Anarchists. You would find a field there." I smiled. "Instinctive Anarchists?" I said, "that means they are unspoiled by preconceived notions, unsophisticated, and receptive. Is that what you mean?"

"Yes, that is what I mean," he replied.

The interview with Gorki left me depressed. Nor was our second meeting more satisfactory on the occasion of my first trip to Moscow. By the same train travelled Radek, Demyan Bedny, the popular Bolshevik versifier, and Zipperovitch, then the president of the Petrograd unions. We found ourselves in the same car, the one reserved for Bolshevik officials and State dignitaries, comfortable and roomy. On the other hand, the "common" man, the non-Communist without influence had literally to fight his way into the always overcrowded railway carriages, provided he had a *propusk* to travel—a most difficult thing to procure.

I spent the time of the journey discussing Russian conditions with Zipperovitch, a kindly man of deep convictions, and with Demyan Bedny, a big coarse-looking man. Radek held forth at length on his experiences in Germany and German prisons.

I learned that Gorki was also on the train, and I was glad of another opportunity for a chat with him when he called to see me. The one thing uppermost in my mind at the moment was an article which had appeared in the Petrograd *Pravda* a few days before my departure. It treated of morally defective children, the writer urging prison for them. Nothing I had heard or seen during my six weeks in Russia so outraged me as this brutal and antiquated attitude toward the child. I was eager to know what Gorki thought of the matter. Of course, he was opposed to prisons for the morally defective, he would advocate reformatories instead. "What do you mean by morally defective?" I asked. "Our young are the result of alcoholism rampant during the Russian-Japanese War, and of syphilis. What except moral defection could result from such a heritage?" he replied. I argued that morality changes with conditions and climate, and that unless one believed in the theory of free will one cannot consider morality a fixed matter. As to children, their sense of responsibility is primitive, and they lack the spirit of social adherence. But Gorki insisted that there was a fearful spread of moral defection among children and that such cases should be isolated.

I then broached the problem that was troubling me most. What about persecution and terror—were all the horrors inevitable, or was there some fault in Bolshevism itself? The Bolsheviki were making mistakes, but they were doing the best they knew how, Gorki said drily. Nothing more could be expected, he thought.

I recalled a certain article by Gorki, published in his paper, *New Life*, which I had read in the Missouri Penitentiary. It was a scathing arraignment of the Bolsheviki. There must have been powerful reasons to change Gorki's point of view so completely. Perhaps he is right. I must wait. I must study the situation; I must get at the facts. Above all, I must see for myself Bolshevism at work.

We spoke of the drama. On my first visit by way of introduction, I had shown Gorki an announcement card of the dramatic course I had given in America. John Galsworthy was among the playwrights I had discussed then. Gorki expressed surprise that I considered Galsworthy an artist. In his opinion Galsworthy could not be compared with Bernard Shaw. I had to differ. I did not underestimate Shaw, but considered Galsworthy the greater artist. I detected irritation in Gorki, and as his hacking cough continued, I broke off the discussion. He soon left. I remained dejected from the interview. It gave me nothing.

When we pulled into the Moscow station my chaperon, Demyan Bedny, had vanished and I was left on the platform with all my traps. Radek came to my rescue. He called a porter, took me and my baggage to his waiting automobile and insisted that I come to his apartments in the Kremlin. There I was graciously received by his wife and invited to dinner served by their maid. After that Radek began the difficult task of getting me quartered in the Hotel National, known as the First House of the Moscow Soviet. With all his influence it required hours to secure a room for me.

Radek's luxurious apartment, the maidservant, the splendid dinner seemed strange in Russia. But the comradely concern of Radek and the hospitality of his wife were grateful to me. Except at the Zorins and the Shatovs I had not met with anything like it. I felt that kindliness, sympathy, and solidarity were still alive in Russia.

CHAPTER IV

MOSCOW: FIRST IMPRESSIONS

COMING from Petrograd to Moscow is like being suddenly transferred from a desert to active life, so great is the contrast. On reaching the large open square in front of the main Moscow station I was amazed at the sight of busy crowds, cabbies, and porters. The same picture presented itself all the way from the station to the Kremlin. The streets were alive with men, women, and children. Almost everybody carried a bundle, or dragged a loaded sleigh. There was life, motion, and movement, quite different from the stillness that oppressed me in Petrograd.

I noticed considerable display of the military in the city, and scores of men dressed in leather suits with guns in their belts. "Tcheka men, our Extraordinary Commission," explained Radek. I had heard of the Tcheka before: Petrograd talked of it with dread and hatred. However, the soldiers and Tchekists were never much in evidence in the city on the Neva. Here in Moscow they seemed everywhere. Their presence reminded me of a remark Jack Reed had made: "Moscow is a military encampment," he had said; "spies everywhere, the bureaucracy most autocratic. I always feel relieved when I get out of Moscow. But, then, Petrograd is a proletarian city and is permeated with the spirit of the Revolution. Moscow always was hierarchical. It is much more so now." I found that Jack Reed was right. Moscow was indeed hierarchical. Still the life was intense, varied, and interesting. What struck me most forcibly, besides the display of militarism, was the preoccupation of the people. There seemed to be no common interest between them. Everyone rushed about as a detached unit in quest of his own, pushing and knocking against everyone else. Repeatedly I saw women or children fall from exhaustion without any one stopping to lend assistance. People stared at me when I would bend over the heap on the slippery pavement or gather up the bundles that had fallen into the street. I spoke to friends about what looked to me like a strange lack of fellow-feeling. They explained it as a result partly of the general distrust and suspicion created by the Tcheka, and partly due to the absorbing task of getting the day's food. One had neither vitality nor feeling left to think of others. Yet there did not seem to be such a scarcity of food as in Petrograd, and the people were warmer and better dressed.

I spent much time on the streets and in the market places. Most of the latter, as also the famous Soukharevka, were in full operation. Occasionally soldiers would raid the markets; but as a rule they were suffered to continue. They presented the most vital and interesting part of the city's life. Here gathered proletarian and aristocrat, Communist and bourgeois, peasant and intellectual. Here they were bound by the common desire to sell and buy, to trade and bargain. Here one could find for sale a rusty iron pot alongside of an exquisite ikon; an old pair of shoes and intricately worked lace; a few yards of cheap calico and a beautiful old Persian shawl. The rich of yesterday, hungry and emaciated, denuding themselves of their last glories; the rich of to-day buying—it was indeed an amazing picture in revolutionary Russia.

Who was buying the finery of the past, and where did the purchasing power come from? The buyers were numerous. In Moscow one was not so limited as to sources of information as in Petrograd; the very streets furnished that source.

The Russian people even after four years of war and three years of revolution remained unsophisticated. They were suspicious of strangers and reticent at first. But when they learned that one had come from America and did not belong to the governing political party, they gradually lost their reserve. Much information I gathered from them and some explanation of the things that perplexed me since my arrival. I talked frequently with the workers and peasants and the women on the markets.

The forces which had led up to the Russian Revolution had remained *terra incognita* to these simple folk, but the Revolution itself had struck deep into their souls. They knew nothing of theories, but they believed that there was to be no more of the hated *barin* (master) and now the *barin* was again upon them. "The *barin* has everything," they would say, "white bread, clothing, even chocolate, while we have nothing." "Communism, equality, freedom," they jeered, "lies and deception."

I would return to the National bruised and battered, my illusions gradually shattered, my foundations crumbling. But I would not let go. After all, I thought, the common people could not understand the tremendous difficulties confronting the Soviet Government: the imperialist forces arraigned against Russia, the many attacks which drained her of her men who otherwise would be employed in productive labour, the blockade which was relentlessly slaying Russia's young and weak. Of course, the people could not understand these things, and I must not be misled by their bitterness born of suffering. I must be patient. I must get to the source of the evils confronting me.

The National, like the Petrograd Astoria, was a former hotel but not nearly in as good condition. No rations were given out there except three quarters of a pound of bread every two days. Instead there was a common dining room where dinners and suppers were served. The meals consisted of soup and a little meat, sometimes fish or pancakes, and tea. In the evening we usually had *kasha* and tea. The food was not too plentiful, but one could exist on it were it not so abominably prepared.

I saw no reason for this spoiling of provisions. Visiting the kitchen I discovered an array of servants controlled by a number of officials, commandants, and inspectors. The kitchen staff were poorly paid; moreover, they were not given the same food served to us. They resented this discrimination and their interest was not in their work. This situation resulted in much graft and waste, criminal in the face of the general scarcity of food. Few of the tenants of the National, I learned, took their meals in the common dining room. They prepared or had their meals prepared by servants in a separate kitchen set aside for that purpose. There, as in the Astoria, I found the same scramble for a place on the stove, the same bickering and quarrelling, the same greedy, envious watching of each other. Was that Communism in action, I wondered. I heard the usual explanation: Yudenitch, Denikin, Kolchak, the blockade— but the stereotyped phrases no longer satisfied me.

Before I left Petrograd Jack Reed said to me: "When you reach Moscow, look up Angelica Balabanova. She will receive you gladly and will put you up should you be unable to find a room." I had heard of Balabanova before, knew of her work, and was naturally anxious to meet her.

A few days after reaching Moscow I called her

up. Would she see me? Yes, at once, though she was not feeling well. I found Balabanova in a small, cheerless room, lying huddled up on the sofa. She was not prepossessing but for her eyes, large and luminous, radiating sympathy and kindness. She received me most graciously, like an old friend, and immediately ordered the inevitable samovar. Over our tea we talked of America, the labour movement there, our deportation, and finally about Russia. I put to her the questions I had asked many Communists regarding the contrasts and discrepancies which confronted me at every step. She surprised me by not giving the usual excuses; she was the first who did not repeat the old refrain. She did refer to the scarcity of food, fuel, and clothing which was responsible for much of the graft and corruption; but on the whole she thought life itself mean and limited. " A rock on which the highest hopes are shattered. Life thwarts the best intentions and breaks the finest spirits." she said. Rather an unusual view for a Marxian, a Communist, and one in the thick of the battle. I knew she was then secretary of the Third International. Here was a personality, one who was not a mere echo, one who felt deeply the complexity of the

Russian situation. I went away profoundly impressed, and attracted by her sad, luminous eyes.

I soon discovered that Balabanova—or Balabanoff, as she preferred to be called—was at the beck and call of everybody. Though poor in health and engaged in many functions, she yet found time to minister to the needs of her legion callers. Often she went without necessaries herself, giving away her own rations, always busy trying to secure medicine or some little delicacy for the sick and suffering. Her special concern were the stranded Italians of whom there were quite a number in Petrograd and Moscow. Balabanova had lived and worked in Italy for many years until she almost became Italian herself. She felt deeply with them, who were as far away from their native soil as from events in Russia. She was their friend, their advisor, their main support in a world of strife and struggle. Not only the Italians but almost everyone else was the concern of this remarkable little woman: no one needed a Communist membership card to Angelica's heart. No wonder some of her comrades considered her a "senti mentalist who wasted her precious time in philanthropy." Many verbal battles I had on this score with the type of Communist who had become callous and hard, altogether barren of the qualities which characterized the Russian idealist of the past.

Similar criticism as of Balabanova I heard expressed of another leading Communist, Lunacharsky. Already in Petrograd I was told sneeringly, "Lunacharsky is a scatterbrain who wastes millions on foolish ventures." But I was eager to meet the man who was the Commissar of one of the important departments in Russia, that of education. Presently an opportunity presented itself.

The Kremlin, the old citadel of Tsardom, I found heavily guarded and inaccessible to the "common" man. But I had come by appointment and in the company of a man who had an admission card, and therefore passed the guard without trouble. We soon reached the Lunacharsky apartments, situated in an old quaint building within the walls. Though the reception room was crowded with people waiting to be admitted, Lunacharsky called me in as soon as I was announced.

His greeting was very cordial. Did I "intend to remain a free bird" was one of his first questions, or would I be willing to join him in his work? I was rather surprised. Why should one have to give up his freedom, especially in educational work? Were not initiative and freedom essential? However, I had come to learn from Lunacharsky about the revolutionary system of education in Russia, of which we had heard so much in America. I was especially interested in the care the children were receiving. The Moscow *Pravda*, like the Petrograd newspapers, had been agitated by a controversy about the treatment of the morally defective. I expressed surprise at such an attitude in Soviet Russia. "Of course, it is all barbarous and antiquated," Lunacharsky said, "and I am fighting it tooth and nail. The sponsors of prisons for children are old criminal jurists, still imbued with Tsarist methods. I have organized a commission of physicians, pedagogues, and psychologists to deal with this question. Of course, those children must not be punished." I felt tremendously relieved. Here at last was a man who had gotten away from the cruel old methods of punishment. I told him of the splendid work done in capitalist America by Judge Lindsay and of some of the experimental schools for backward children. Lunacharsky was much interested. "Yes, that is just what we want here, the American system of education," he exclaimed. "You surely do not mean the American public school system?" I asked. "You know of the insurgent movement in America against our public school method of education, the work done by Professor Dewey and others?" Lunacharsky had heard little about it. Russia had been so long cut off from the western world and there was great lack of books on modern education. He was eager to learn of the new ideas and methods. I sensed in Lunacharsky a personality full of faith and devotion to the Revolution, one who was carrying on the great work of education in a physically and spiritually difficult environment.

He suggested the calling of a conference of teachers if I would talk to them about the new tendencies in education in America, to which I readily consented. Schools and other institutions in his charge were to be visited later. I left Lunacharsky filled with new hope. I would join him in his work, I thought. What greater service could one render the Russian people?

During my visit to Moscow I saw Lunacharsky several times. He was always the same kindly gracious man, but I soon began to notice that he was being handicapped in his work by forces within his own party: most of his good intentions and decisions never saw the light. Evidently Lunacharsky was caught in the same machine that apparently held everything in its iron grip. What was that machine? Who directed its movements?

Although the control of visitors at the National was very strict, no one being able to go in or out without a special *propusk* [permit], men and women of different political factions managed to call on me: Anarchists, Left Social Revolutionists, Coöperators, and people I had known in America and who had returned to Russia to play their part in the Revolution. They had come with deep faith and high hope, but I found almost all of them discouraged, some even embittered. Though widely differing in their political views, nearly all of my callers related an identical story, the story of the high tide of the Revolution, of the wonderful spirit that led the people forward, of the possibilities of the masses, the rôle of the Bolsheviki as the spokesmen of the most extreme revolutionary slogans and their betrayal of the Revolution after they had secured power. All spoke of the Brest Litovsk peace as the beginning of the downward march. The Left Social Revolutionists especially, men of culture and earnestness, who had suffered much under the Tsar and now saw their hopes and aspirations thwarted, were most emphatic in their condemnation. They supported their statements by evidence of the havoc wrought by the methods of forcible requisition and the punitive expeditions to the villages, of the abyss created between town and country, the hatred engendered between peasant and worker. They told of the persecution of their comrades, the shooting of innocent men and women, the criminal inefficiency, waste, and destruction.

How, then, could the Bolsheviki maintain themselves in power? After all, they were only a small minority, about five hundred thousand members as an exaggerated estimate. The Russian masses, I was told, were exhausted by hunger and cowed by terrorism. Moreover, they had lost faith in all parties and ideas. Nevertheless, there were frequent peasant uprisings in various parts of Russia, but these were ruthlessly quelled. There were also constant strikes in Moscow, Petrograd, and other industrial centres, but the censorship was so rigid little ever became known to the masses at large.

I sounded my visitors on intervention. "We want none of outside interference," was the

felt that they could not publicly even speak out against them so long as Russia was being attacked, much less fight their régime. "Have not their tactics and methods been imposed on the Bolsheviki by intervention and blockade?" I argued. "Only partly so," was the reply. "Most of their methods spring from their lack of understanding of the character and the needs of the Russian people and the mad obsession of dictatorship, which is not even the dictatorship of the proletariat but the dictatorship of a small group *over* the proletariat."

When I broached the subject of the People's Soviets and the elections my visitors smiled. "Elections! There are no such things in Russia, unless you call threats and terrorism elections. It is by these alone that the Bolsheviki secure a majority. A few Mensheviki, Social Revolutionists, or Anarchists are permitted to slip into the Soviets, but they have not the shadow of a chance to be heard."

The picture painted looked black and dismal. Still I clung to my faith.

CHAPTER V

MEETING PEOPLE

AT A conference of the Moscow Anarchists
in March I first learned of the part some
Anarchists had played in the Russian
Revolution. In the July uprising of 1917 the
Kronstadt sailors were led by the Anarchist
Yarchuck; the Constituent Assembly was dis-
persed by Zhelezniakov; the Anarchists had
participated on every front and helped to drive
back the Allied attacks. It was the consensus
of opinion that the Anarchists were always
among the first to face fire, as they were also the
most active in the reconstructive work. One of
the biggest factories near Moscow, which did not
stop work during the entire period of the Revolution, was managed by an Anarchist. Anarchists
were doing important work in the Foreign Office
and in all other departments. I learned that
the Anarchists had virtually helped the Bolsheviki into power. Five months later, in April,
1918, machine guns were used to destroy the

Moscow Anarchist Club and to suppress their press. That was before Mirbach arrived in Moscow. The field had to be "cleared of disturbing elements," and the Anarchists were the first to suffer. Since then the persecution of the Anarchists has never ceased.

The Moscow Anarchist Conference was critical not only toward the existing régime, but toward its own comrades as well. It spoke frankly of the negative sides of the movement, and of its lack of unity and coöperation during the revolutionary period. Later I was to learn more of the internal dissensions in the Anarchist movement. Before closing, the Conference decided to call on the Soviet Government to release the imprisoned Anarchists and to legalize Anarchist educational work. The Conference asked Alexander Berkman and myself to sign the resolution to that effect. It was a shock to me that Anarchists should ask any government to legalize their efforts, but I still believed the Soviet Government to be at least to some extent expressive of the Revolution. I signed the resolution, and as I was to see Lenin in a few days I promised to take the matter up with him.

The interview with Lenin was arranged by Balabanova. "You must see Ilitch, talk to him about the things that are disturbing you and the work you would like to do," she had said. But some time passed before the opportunity came. At last one day Balabanova called up to ask whether I could go at once. Lenin had sent his car and we were quickly driven over to the Kremlin, passed without question by the guards, and at last ushered into the workroom of the all-powerful president of the People's Commissars.

When we entered Lenin held a copy of the brochure *Trial and Speeches* * in his hands. I had given my only copy to Balabanova, who had evidently sent the booklet on ahead of us to Lenin. One of his first questions was, "When could the Social Revolution be expected in America?" I had been asked the question repeatedly before, but I was astounded to hear it from Lenin. It seemed incredible that a man of his information should know so little about conditions in America.

My Russian at this time was halting, but Lenin declared that though he had lived in Europe for many years he had not learned to speak foreign languages: the conversation would therefore have to be carried on in Russian. At

* *Trial and Speeches of Alexander Berkman and Emma Goldman before the Federal Court of New York, June-July, 1917.* Mother Earth Publishing Co., New York.

once he launched into a eulogy of our speeches in court. "What a splendid opportunity for propaganda," he said; "it is worth going to prison, if the courts can so successfully be turned into a forum." I felt his steady cold gaze upon me, penetrating my very being, as if he were reflecting upon the use I might be put to. Presently he asked what I would want to do. I told him I would like to repay America what it had done for Russia. I spoke of the Society of the Friends of Russian Freedom, organized thirty years ago by George Kennan and later reorganized by Alice Stone Blackwell and other liberal Americans. I briefly sketched the splendid work they had done to arouse interest in the struggle for Russian freedom, and the great moral and financial aid the Society had given through all those years. To organize a Russian society for American freedom was my plan. Lenin appeared enthusiastic. "That is a great idea, and you shall have all the help you want. But, of course, it will be under the auspices of the Third International. Prepare your plan in writing and send it to me."

I broached the subject of the Anarchists in Russia. I showed him a letter I had received from Martens, the Soviet representative in

America, shortly before my deportation. Martens asserted that the Anarchists in Russia enjoyed full freedom of speech and press. Since my arrival I found scores of Anarchists in prison and their press suppressed. I explained that I could not think of working with the Soviet Government so long as my comrades were in prison for opinion's sake. I also told him of the resolutions of the Moscow Anarchist Conference. He listened patiently and promised to bring the matter to the attention of his party. "But as to free speech," he remarked, "that is, of course, a bourgeois notion. There can be no free speech in a revolutionary period. We have the peasantry against us because we can give them nothing in return for their bread. We will have them on our side when we have something to exchange. Then you can have all the free speech you want —but not now. Recently we needed peasants to cart some wood into the city. They demanded salt. We thought we had no salt, but then we discovered seventy poods in Moscow in one of our warehouses. At once the peasants were willing to cart the wood. Your comrades must wait until we can meet the needs of the peasants. Meanwhile, they should work with us. Look at William Shatov, for instance, who has helped save Petrograd from Yudenitch. He works with us and we appreciate his services. Shatov was among the first to receive the order of the Red Banner."

Free speech, free press, the spiritual achievements of centuries, what were they to this man? A Puritan, he was sure his scheme alone could redeem Russia. Those who served his plans were right, the others could not be tolerated.

A shrewd Asiatic, this Lenin. He knows how to play on the weak sides of men by flattery, rewards, medals. I left convinced that his approach to people was purely utilitarian, for the use he could get out of them for his scheme. And his scheme—was it the Revolution?

I prepared the plan for the Society of the Russian Friends of American Freedom and elaborated the details of the work I had in mind, but refused to place myself under the protecting wing of the Third International. I explained to Lenin that the American people had little faith in politics, and would certainly consider it an imposition to be directed and guided by a political machine from Moscow. I could not consistently align myself with the Third International.

Some time later I saw Tchicherin. I believe it was 4 A. M. when our interview took place.

He also asked about the possibilities of a revolution in America, and seemed to doubt my judgment when I informed him that there was no hope of it in the near future. We spoke of the I. W. W., which had evidently been misrepresented to him. I assured Tchicherin that while I am not an I. W. W. I must state that they represented the only conscious and effective revolutionary proletarian organization in the United States, and were sure to play an important rôle in the future labour history of the country.

Next to Balabanova, Tchicherin impressed me as the most simple and unassuming of the leading Communists in Moscow. But all were equally naïve in their estimate of the world outside of Russia. Was their judgment so faulty because they had been cut off from Europe and America so long? Or was their great need of European help father to their wish? At any rate, they all clung to the idea of approaching revolutions in the western countries, forgetful that revolutions are not made to order, and apparently unconscious that their own revolution had been twisted out of shape and semblance and was gradually being done to death.

The editor of the London *Daily Herald*, accompanied by one of his reporters, had preceded me to Moscow. They wanted to visit Kropotkin, and they had been given a special car. Together with Alexander Berkman and A. Shapiro, I was able to join Mr. Lansbury.

The Kropotkin cottage stood back in the garden away from the street. Only a faint ray from a kerosene lamp lit up the path to the house. Kropotkin received us with his characteristic graciousness, evidently glad at our visit. But I was shocked at his altered appearance. The last time I had seen him was in 1907, in Paris, which I visited after the Anarchist Congress in Amsterdam. Kropotkin, barred from France for many years, had just been given the right to return. He was then sixty-five years of age, but still so full of life and energy that he seemed much younger. Now he looked old and worn.

I was eager to get some light from Kropotkin on the problems that were troubling me, particularly on the relation of the Bolsheviki to the Revolution. What was his opinion? Why had he been silent so long?

I took no notes and therefore I can give only the gist of what Kropotkin said. He stated that the Revolution had carried the people to great spiritual heights and had paved the way for profound social changes. If the people had been permitted to apply their released energies, Russia would not be in her present condition of ruin. The Bolsheviki, who had been carried to the top by the revolutionary wave, first caught the popular ear by extreme revolutionary slogans, thereby gaining the confidence of the masses and the support of militant revolutionists.

He continued to narrate that early in the October period the Bolsheviki began to subordinate the interests of the Revolution to the establishment of their dictatorship, which coerced and paralysed every social activity. He stated that the coöperatives were the main medium that could have bridged the interests of the peasants and the workers. The coöperatives were among the first to be crushed. He spoke with much feeling of the oppression, the persecution, the hounding of every shade of opinion, and cited numerous instances of the misery and distress of the people. He emphasized that the Bolsheviki had discredited Socialism and Communism in the eyes of the Russian people.

"Why haven't you raised your voice against these evils, against this machine that is sapping the life blood of the Revolution?" I asked. He gave two reasons. As long as Russia was being attacked by the combined Imperialists, and Russian women and children were dying from the effects of the blockade, he could not join the shrieking chorus of the ex-revolutionists in the cry of "Crucify!" He preferred silence. Secondly, there was no medium of expression in Russia itself. To protest to the Government was useless. Its concern was to maintain itself in power. It could not stop at such "trifles" as human rights or human lives. Then he added: "We have always pointed out the effects of Marxism in action. Why be surprised now?"

I asked Kropotkin whether he was noting down his impressions and observations. Surely he must see the importance of such a record to his comrades and to the workers; in fact, to the whole world. "No," he said; "it is impossible to write when one is in the midst of great human suffering, when every hour brings new tragedies. Then there may be a raid at any moment. The Tcheka comes swooping down in the night, ransacks every corner, turns everything inside out, and marches off with every scrap of paper. Under such constant stress it is impossible to keep records. But besides these considerations there is my book on Ethics.   I can only work a few hours a day, and I must concentrate on that to the exclusion of everything else."

After a tender embrace which Peter never failed to give those he loved, we returned to our car.   My heart was heavy, my spirit confused and troubled by what I had heard.   I was also distressed by the poor state of health of our comrade: I feared he could not survive till spring. The thought that Peter Kropotkin might go to his grave and that the world might never know what he thought of the Russian Revolution was appalling.

CHAPTER VI

PREPARING FOR AMERICAN DEPORTEES

EVENTS in Moscow, quickly following each other, were full of interest. I wanted to remain in that vital city, but as I had left all my effects in Petrograd I decided to return there and then come back to Moscow to join Lunacharsky in his work. A few days before my departure a young woman, an Anarchist, came to visit me. She was from the Petrograd Museum of the Revolution and she called to inquire whether I would take charge of the Museum branch work in Moscow. She explained that the original idea of the Museum was due to the famous old revolutionist Vera Nikolaievna Figner, and that it had recently been organized by non-partisan elements. The majority of the men and women who worked in the Museum were not Communists, she said; but they were devoted to the Revolution and anxious to create something which could in the future serve as a source of information and in-

57

spiration to earnest students of the great Russian Revolution. When my caller was informed that I was about to return to Petrograd, she invited me to visit the Museum and to become acquainted with its work.

Upon my arrival in Petrograd I found unexpected work awaiting me. Zorin informed me that he had been notified by Tchicherin that a thousand Russians had been deported from America and were on their way to Russia. They were to be met at the border and quarters were to be immediately prepared for them in Petrograd. Zorin asked me to join the Commission about to be organized for that purpose.

The plan of such a commission for American deportees had been broached to Zorin soon after our arrival in Russia. At that time Zorin directed us to talk the matter over with Tchicherin, which we did. But three months passed without anything having been done about it. Meanwhile, our comrades of the *Buford* were still walking from department to department, trying to be placed where they might do some good. They were a sorry lot, those men who had come to Russia with such high hopes, eager to render service to the revolutionary people. Most of them were skilled workers, mechanics—

men Russia needed badly; but the cumbersome Bolshevik machine and general inefficiency made it a very complex matter to put them to work. Some had tried independently to secure jobs, but they could accomplish very little. Moreover, those who found employment were soon made to feel that the Russian workers resented the eagerness and intensity of their brothers from America. "Wait till you have starved as long as we," they would say, "wait till you have tasted the blessings of Commissarship, and we will see if you are still so eager." In every way the deportees were discouraged and their enthusiasm dampened.

To avoid this unnecessary waste of energy and suffering the Commission was at last organized in Petrograd. It consisted of Ravitch, the then Minister of Internal Affairs for the Northern District; her secretary, Kaplun; two members of the Bureau of War Prisoners; Alexander Berkman, and myself. The new deportees were due in two weeks, and much work was to be done to prepare for their reception. It was unfortunate that no active participation could be expected from Ravitch because her time was too much occupied. Besides holding the post of Minister of the Interior she was Chief of the

Petrograd Militia, and she also represented the
Moscow Foreign Office in Petrograd. Her regular working hours were from 8 A. M. to 2 A. M.
Kaplun, a very able administrator, had charge
of the entire internal work of the Department
and could therefore give us very little of his time.
There remained only four persons to accomplish
within a short time the big task of preparing living quarters for a thousand deportees in starved
and ruined Russia. Moreover, Alexander Berkman, heading the Reception Committee, had
to leave for the Latvian border to meet the
exiles.

It was an almost impossible task for one per-
son, but I was very anxious to save the second
group of deportees the bitter experiences and the
disappointments of my fellow companions of the
Buford. I could undertake the work only by
making the condition that I be given the right of
entry to the various government departments,
for I had learned by that time how paralysing
was the effect of the bureaucratic red tape which
delayed and often frustrated the most earnest
and energetic efforts. Kaplun consented. "Call
on me at any time for anything you may re-
quire," he said; "I will give orders that you be
admitted everywhere and supplied with every-

the police before, I informed him; why should I do so in revolutionary Russia? "In bourgeois countries that is a different matter," explained Kaplun; "with us the Tcheka defends the Revolution and fights sabotage." I started on my work determined to do without the Tcheka. Surely there must be other methods, I thought.

Then began a chase over Petrograd. Materials were very scarce and it was most difficult to procure them owing to the unbelievably centralized Bolshevik methods. Thus to get a pound of nails one had to file applications in about ten or fifteen bureaus; to secure some bed linen or ordinary dishes one wasted days. Everywhere in the offices crowds of Government employees stood about smoking cigarettes, awaiting the hour when the tedious task of the day would be over. My co-workers of the War Prisoners' Bureau fumed at the irritating and unnecessary delays, but to no purpose. They threatened with the Tcheka, with the concentration camp, even with *raztrel* (shooting). The latter was the most favourite argument. Whenever any difficulty arose one immediately heard *raztreliat*— to be shot. But the expression, so terrible in its significance, was gradually losing its effect upon the people: man gets used to everything.

I decided to try other methods. I would talk to the employees in the departments about the vital interest the conscious American workers felt in the great Russian Revolution, and of their faith and hope in the Russian proletariat. The people would become interested immediately, but the questions they would ask were as strange as they were pitiful: "Have the people enough to eat in America? How soon will the Revolution be there? Why did you come to starving Russia?" They were eager for information and news, these mentally and physically starved people, cut off by the barbarous blockade from all touch with the western world. Things American were something wonderful to them. A piece of chocolate or a cracker were unheard-of dainties—they proved the key to everybody's heart.

Within two weeks I succeeded in procuring most of the things needed for the expected deportees, including furniture, linen, and dishes. A miracle, everybody said.

However, the renovation of the houses that were to serve as living quarters for the exiles was not accomplished so easily. I inspected what, found them located in the former prostitute district; cheap dives they were, until the Bolsheviki closed all brothels. They were germ-eaten, ill-smelling, and filthy. It was no small problem to turn those dark holes into a fit habitation within two weeks. A coat of paint was a luxury not to be thought of. There was nothing else to do but to strip the rooms of furniture and draperies, and have them thoroughly cleaned and disinfected.

One morning a group of forlorn-looking creatures, in charge of two militiamen, were brought to my temporary office. They came to work, I was informed. The group consisted of a one-armed old man, a consumptive woman, and eight boys and girls, mere children, pale, starved, and in rags. "Where do these unfortunates come from?" I inquired. "They are speculators," one of the militiamen replied; "we rounded them up on the market." The prisoners began to weep. They were no speculators, they protested; they were starving, they had received no bread in two days. They were compelled to go out to the market to sell matches or thread to secure a little bread. In the midst of this scene the old man fainted from exhaustion, demonstrating better than words that he had speculated only in hunger. I had seen such "speculators" before, driven in groups through the streets of Moscow and Petrograd by convoys with loaded guns pointed at the backs of the prisoners.

I could not think of having the work done by these starved creatures. But the militiamen insisted that they would not let them go; they had orders to make them work. I called up Kaplun and informed him that I considered it out of the question to have quarters for American deportees prepared by Russian convicts whose only crime was hunger. Thereupon Kaplun ordered the group set free and consented that I give them of the bread sent for the workers' rations. But a valuable day was lost.

The next morning a group of boys and girls came singing along the Nevski Prospekt. They were *kursanti* from the Tauride Palace who were sent to my office to work. On my first visit to the palace I had been shown the quarters of the *kursanti*, the students of the Bolshevik academy. They were mostly village boys and girls housed, fed, clothed, and educated by the Government, later to be placed in responsible positions in the Soviet régime. At the time I was impressed by the institutions, but by April I had looked somewhat beneath the surface. I recalled what a young woman, a Communist, had told me in Moscow about these students. "They are the special caste now being reared in Russia," she had said. "Like the church which maintains and educates its religious priesthood, our Government trains a military and civic priesthood. They are a favoured lot." I had more than one occasion to convince myself of the truth of it. The *kursanti* were being given every advantage and many special privileges. They knew their importance and they behaved accordingly.

Their first demand when they came to me was for the extra rations of bread they had been promised. This demand satisfied, they stood about and seemed to have no idea of work. It was evident that whatever else the *kursanti* might be taught, it was not to labour. But, then, few people in Russia know how to work. The situation looked hopeless. Only ten days remained till the arrival of the deportees, and the "hotels" assigned for their use were still in as uninhabitable a condition as before. It was no use to threaten with the Tcheka, as my co-workers did. I appealed to the boys and girls in the spirit of the American deportees who were about to arrive in Russia full of enthusiasm for the Revolution and eager to join in the great work of reconstruction.   The *kursanti* were the pampered charges of the Government, but they were not long from the villages, and they had had no time to become corrupt.   My appeal was effective.   They took up the work with a will, and at the end of ten days the three famous hotels were ready as far as willingness to work and hot water without soap could make them.   We were very proud of our achievement and we eagerly awaited the arrival of the deportees.

At last they came, but to our great surprise they proved to be no deportees at all.   They were Russian war prisoners from Germany.   The misunderstanding was due to the blunder of some official in Tchicherin's office who misread the radio information about the party due at the border.   The prepared hotels were locked and sealed; they were not to be used for the returned war prisoners because "they were prepared for American deportees who still might come."   All the efforts and labour had been in vain.

CHAPTER VII

REST HOMES FOR WORKERS

SINCE my return from Moscow I noticed a change in Zorin's attitude: he was reserved, distant, and not as friendly as when we first met. I ascribed it to the fact that he was overworked and fatigued, and not wishing to waste his valuable time I ceased visiting the Zorins as frequently as before. One day, however, he called up to ask if Alexander Berkman and myself would join him in certain work he was planning, and which was to be done in hurry-up American style, as he put it. On calling to see him we found him rather excited—an unusual thing for Zorin who was generally quiet and reserved. He was full of a new scheme to build "rest homes" for workers. He explained that on Kameniy Ostrov were the magnificent mansions of the Stolypins, the Polovtsovs, and others of the aristocracy and bourgeoisie, and that he was planning to turn them into recreation centres for workers. Would we join in the work?

Of course, we consented eagerly, and the next morning we went over to inspect the island.   It was indeed an ideal spot, dotted with magnificent mansions, some of them veritable museums, containing rare gems of painting, tapestry, and furniture.   The man in charge of the buildings called our attention to the art treasures, protesting that they would be injured or entirely destroyed if put to the planned use.   But Zorin was set on his scheme.   "Recreation homes for workers are more important than art," he said.

We returned to the Astoria determined to devote ourselves to the work and to go at it intensively, as the houses were to be ready for the First of May.   We prepared detailed plans for dining rooms, sleeping chambers, reading rooms, theatre and lecture halls, and recreation places for the workers.   As the first and most necessary step we proposed the organization of a dining room to feed the workers who were to be employed in preparing the place for their comrades.   I had learned from my previous experience with the hotels that much valuable time was lost because of the failure to provide for those actually employed on such work.   Zorin consented and promised that we were to take charge within a few days.   But a week passed and nothing further was heard about what was to be a rush job. Some time later Zorin called up to ask us to accompany him to the island. On our arrival there we found half-a-dozen Commissars already in charge, with scores of people idling about. Zorin reassured us that matters would arrange themselves and that we should have an opportunity to organize the work as planned. However, we soon realized that the newly fledged officialdom was as hard to cope with as the old bureaucracy.

Every Commissar had his favourites whom he managed to list as employed on the job, thereby entitling them to bread rations and a meal. Thus almost before any actual workers appeared on the scene, eighty alleged "technicians" were already in possession of dinner tickets and bread cards. The men actually mobilized for the work received hardly anything. The result was general sabotage. Most of the men sent over to prepare the rest homes for the workers came from concentration camps: they were convicts and military deserters. I had often watched them at work, and in justice to them it must be said that they did not overexert themselves. "Why should we," they would say; "we are fed on Sovietski soup; dirty dishwater it is, and we

receive only what is left over from the idlers who
order us about. And who will rest in these
homes? Not we or our brothers in the factories.
Only those who belong to the party or who have
a pull will enjoy this place. Besides, the spring
is near; we are needed at home on the farm.
Why are we kept here?" Indeed, they did not
exert themselves, those stalwart sons of Russia's soil. There was no incentive: they had no
point of contact with the life about them, and
there was no one who could translate to them the
meaning of work in revolutionary Russia. They
were dazed by war, revolution, and hunger—
nothing could rouse them out of their stupor.

Many of the buildings on Kameniy Ostrov
had been taken up for boarding schools and
homes for defectives; some were occupied by old
professors, teachers, and other intellectuals. Since
the Revolution these people lived there un-
molested, but now orders came to vacate, to
make room for the rest homes. As almost no
provision had been made to supply the dis-
possessed ones with other quarters, they were
practically forced into the streets. Those friendly
with Zinoviev, Gorki, or other influential Communists took their troubles to them, but persons lacking "pull" found no redress. The

scenes of misery which I was compelled to witness daily exhausted my energies. It was all unnecessarily cruel, impractical, without any bearing on the Revolution. Added to this was the chaos and confusion which prevailed. The bureaucratic officials seemed to take particular delight in countermanding each other's orders. Houses already in the process of renovation, and on which much work and material were spent, would suddenly be left unfinished and some other work begun. Mansions filled with art treasures were turned into night lodgings, and dirty iron cots put among antique furniture and oil paintings—an incongruous, stupid waste of time and energy. Zorin would frequently hold consultations by the hour with the staff of artists and engineers making plans for theatres, lecture halls, and amusement places, while the Commissars sabotaged the work. I stood the painful and ridiculous situation for two weeks, then gave up the matter in despair.

Early in May the workers' rest homes on Kameniy Ostrov were opened with much pomp, music, and speeches. Glowing accounts were sent broadcast of the marvellous things done for the workers in Russia. In reality, it was Coney Island transferred to the environs of Petrograd, a gaudy showplace for credulous visitors. From that time on Zorin's demeanour to me changed. He became cold, even antagonistic. No doubt he began to sense the struggle which was going on within me, and the break which was bound to come. I did, however, see much of Lisa Zorin, who had just become a mother. I nursed her and her baby glad of the opportunity thus to express my gratitude for the warm friendship the Zorins had shown me during my first months in Russia. I appreciated their sterling honesty and devotion. Both were so favourably placed politically that they could be supplied with everything they wanted, yet Lisa Zorin lacked the simplest garments for her baby. "Thousands of Russian working women have no more, and why should I?" Lisa would say. When she was so weak that she could not nurse her baby, Zorin could not be induced to ask for special rations. I had to conspire against them by buying eggs and butter on the market to save the lives of mother and child. But their fine quality of character made my inner struggle the more difficult. Reason urged me to look the social facts in the face. My personal attachment to the Communists I had learned to know and esteem refused to accept the facts. Never

CHAPTER VIII

THE FIRST OF MAY IN PETROGRAD

IN 1890 the First of May was for the first time
celebrated in America as Labour's international holiday. May Day became to me a
great, inspiring event. To witness the celebration of the First of May in a free country—it was
something to dream of, to long for, but perhaps
never to be realized. And now, in 1920, the
dream of many years was about to become real
in revolutionary Russia. I could hardly await
the morning of May First. It was a glorious
day, with the warm sun melting away the last
crust of the hard winter. Early in the morning
strains of music greeted me: groups of workers
and soldiers were marching through the streets,
singing revolutionary songs. The city was gaily
decorated: the Uritski Square, facing the Winter
Palace, was a mass of red, the streets near by a
veritable riot of colour. Great crowds were about,
all wending their way to the Field of Mars where
the heroes of the Revolution were buried.

74

Though I had an admission card to the reviewing stand I preferred to remain among the people, to feel myself a part of the great hosts that had brought about the world event. This was their day—the day of their making. Yet—they seemed peculiarly quiet, oppressively silent. There was no joy in their singing, no mirth in their laughter. Mechanically they marched, automatically they responded to the claqueurs on the reviewing stand shouting "Hurrah" as the columns passed.

In the evening a pageant was to take place. Long before the appointed hour the Uritski Square down to the palace and to the banks of the Neva was crowded with people gathered to witness the open-air performance symbolizing the triumph of the people. The play consisted of three parts, the first portraying the conditions which led up to the war and the rôle of the German Socialists in it; the second reproduced the February Revolution, with Kerensky in power; the last—the October Revolution. It was a play beautifully set and powerfully acted, a play vivid, real, fascinating. It was given on the steps of the former Stock Exchange, facing the Square. On the highest step sat kings and queens with their courtiers, attended by soldiery in gay uniforms. The scene represents a gala court affair: the announcement is made that a monument is to be built in honour of world capitalism. There is much rejoicing, and a wild orgy of music and dance ensues. Then from the depths there emerge the enslaved and toiling masses, their chains ringing mournfully to the music above. They are responding to the command to build the monument for their masters: some are seen carrying hammers and anvils; others stagger under the weight of huge blocks of stone and loads of brick. The workers are toiling in their world of misery and darkness, lashed to greater effort by the whip of the slave drivers, while above there is light and joy, and the masters are feasting. The completion of the monument is signalled by large yellow disks hoisted on high amidst the rejoicing of the world on top.

At this moment a little red flag is seen waving below, and a small figure is haranguing the people. Angry fists are raised and then flag and figure disappear, only to reappear again in different parts of the underworld. Again the red flag waves, now here. now there. The people slowly gain confidence and presently become threatening. Indignation and anger grow—the

ing, and the workers are slaving. The members of the Second International attend the confab of the mighty. They remain deaf to the plea of the workers to save them from the horrors of war. Then the strains of "God Save the King" announce the arrival of the English army. It is followed by Russian soldiers with machine guns and artillery, and a procession of nurses and cripples, the tribute to the Moloch of war.

The next act pictures the February Revolution. Red flags appear everywhere armed motor cars dash about. The people storm the Winter Palace and haul down the emblem of Tsardom. The Kerensky Government assumes control, and the people are driven back to war. Then comes the marvellous scene of the October Revolution, with soldiers and sailors galloping along the open space before the white marble building. They dash up the steps into the palace, there is a brief struggle, and the victors are hailed by the masses in wild jubilation. The "Internationale" floats upon the air; it mounts higher and higher into exultant peals of joy.

Russia is free—the workers, sailors, and soldiers usher in the new era, the beginning of the world commune!

Tremendously stirring was the picture. But the vast mass remained silent. Only a faint applause was heard from the great throng. I was dumbfounded. How explain this astonishing lack of response? When I spoke to Lisa Zorin about it she said that the people had actually lived through the October Revolution, and that the performance necessarily fell flat by comparison with the reality of 1917. But my little Communist neighbour gave a different version. "The people had suffered so many disappointments since October, 1917," she said, "that the Revolution has lost all meaning to them. The play had the effect of making their disappointment more poignant."

CHAPTER IX

INDUSTRIAL MILITARIZATION

THE Ninth Congress of the All-Russian Communist Party, held in March, 1920, was characterized by a number of measures which meant a complete turn to the right. Foremost among them was the militarization of labour and the establishment of one-man management of industry, as against the collegiate shop system. Obligatory labour had long been a law upon the statutes of the Socialist Republic, but it was carried out, as Trotsky said, "only in a small private way." Now the law was to be made effective in earnest. Russia was to have a militarized industrial army to fight economic disorganization, even as the Red Army had conquered on the various fronts. Such an army could be whipped into line only by rigid discipline, it was claimed. The factory collegiate system had to make place for military industrial management.

The measure was bitterly fought at the Congress by the Communist minority, but party discipline prevailed. However, the excitement did not abate: discussion of the subject continued long after the congress adjourned. Many of the younger Communists agreed that the measure indicated a step to the right, but they defended the decision of their party. "The collegiate system has proven a failure," they said. "The workers will not work voluntarily, and our industry must be revived if we are to survive another year."

Jack Reed also held this view. He had just returned after a futile attempt to reach America through Latvia, and for days we argued about the new policy. Jack insisted it was unavoidable so long as Russia was being attacked and blockaded. "We have been compelled to mobilize an army to fight our external enemies, why not an army to fight our worst internal enemy, hunger? We can do it only by putting our industry on its feet." I pointed out the danger of the military method and questioned whether the workers could be expected to become efficient or to work intensively under compulsion. Still, Jack thought mobilization of labour unavoidable. "It must be tried, anyhow," he said.

of strikes. The story made the rounds that Zinoviev and his staff, while visiting the factories to explain the new policies, were driven by the workers from the premises. To learn about the situation at first hand I decided to visit the factories. Already during my first months in Russia I had asked Zorin for permission to see them. Lisa Zorin had requested me to address some labour meetings, but I declined because I felt that it would be presumptuous on my part to undertake to teach those who had made the revolution. Besides, I was not quite at home with the Russian language then. But when I asked Zorin to let me visit some factories, he was evasive. After I had become acquainted with Ravitch I approached her on the subject, and she willingly consented.

The first works to be visited were the Putilov, the largest and most important engine and car manufacturing establishment. Forty thousand workers had been employed there before the war. Now I was informed that only 7,000 were at work. I had heard much of the Putilovtsi: they had played a heroic part in the revolutionary days and in the defence of Petrograd against Yudenitch.

At the Putilov office we were cordially received, shown about the various departments, and then turned over to a guide. There were four of us in the party, of whom only two could speak Russian. I lagged behind to question a group working at a bench. At first I was met with the usual suspicion, which I overcame by telling the men that I was bringing the greetings of their brothers in America. "And the revolution there?" I was immediately asked. It seemed to have become a national obsession, this idea of a near revolution in Europe and America. Everybody in Russia clung to that hope. It was hard to rob those misinformed people of their naïve faith. "The American revolution is not yet," I told them, "but the Russian Revolution has found an echo among the proletariat in America." I inquired about their work, their lives, and their attitude toward the new decrees "As if we had not been driven enough before," complained one of the men. "Now we are to work under the military *nagaika* [whip]. Of course, we will have to be in the shop or they will punish us as industrial deserters. But how can they get more work out of us? We are suffering hunger and cold. We have no strength to give more." I suggested

Putilov men were receiving the preferred *payok*. "We understand the great misfortune that has befallen Russia," one of the workers replied, "but we cannot squeeze more out of ourselves. Even the two pounds of bread we are getting is not enough. Look at the bread," he said, holding up a black crust; "can we live on that? And our children? If not for our people in the country or some trading on the market we would die altogether. Now comes the new measure which is tearing us away from our people, sending us to the other end of Russia while our brothers from there are going to be dragged here, away from their soil. It's a crazy measure and it won't work."

"But what can the Government do in the face of the food shortage?" I asked. "Food shortage!" the man exclaimed; "look at the markets. Did you see any shortage of food there? Speculation and the new bourgeoisie, that's what's the matter. The one-man management is our new slave driver. First the bourgeoisie sabotaged us, and now they are again in control. But just let them try to boss us! They'll find out. Just let them try!"

The men were bitter and resentful. Presently the guide returned to see what had become of me. He took great pains to explain that industrial conditions in the mill had improved considerably since the militarization of labour went into effect. The men were more content and many more cars had been renovated and engines repaired than within an equal period under the previous management. There were 7,000 productively employed in the works, he assured me. I learned, however, that the real figure was less than 5,000 and that of these only about 2,000 were actual workers. The others were Government officials and clerks.

After the Putilov works we visited the Treugolnik, the great rubber factory of Russia. The place was clean and the machinery in good order—a well-equipped modern plant. When we reached the main workroom we were met by the superintendent, who had been in charge for twenty-five years. He would show us around himself, he said. He seemed to take great pride in the factory, as if it were his own. It rather surprised me that they had managed to keep everything in such fine shape. The guide explained that it

been left in charge. They felt that whatever might happen they must not let the place go to ruin. It was certainly very commendable, I thought, but soon I had occasion to change my mind. At one of the tables, cutting rubber, was an old worker with kindly eyes looking out of a sad, spiritual face. He reminded me of the pilgrim Lucca in Gorki's "Night Lodgings." Our guide kept a sharp vigil, but I managed to slip away while the superintendent was explaining some machinery to the other members of our group.

"Well, *batyushka*, how is it with you?" I greeted the old worker. "Bad, *matushka*," he replied; "times are very hard for us old people." I told him how impressed I was to find everything in such good condition in the shop. "That is so," commented the old worker, "but it is because the superintendent and his staff are hoping from day to day that there may be a change again, and that the Treugolnik will go back to its former owners. I know them. I have worked here long before the German master of this plant put in the new machinery."

Passing through the various rooms of the fac tory I saw the women and girls look up in evident dread. It seemed strange in a country

parently the machines were not the only things that had been carefully watched over—the old discipline, too, had been preserved: the employees thought us Bolshevik inspectors.

The great flour mill of Petrograd, visited next, looked as if it were in a state of siege, with armed soldiers everywhere, even inside the work-rooms. The explanation given was that large quantities of precious flour had been vanishing. The soldiers watched the millmen as if they were galley slaves, and the workers naturally resented such humiliating treatment. They hardly dared to speak. One young chap, a fine-looking fellow, complained to me of the conditions. "We are here virtual prisoners," he said; "we cannot make a step without permission. We are kept hard at work eight hours with only ten minutes for our *kipyatok* [boiled water] and we are searched on leaving the mill." "Is not the theft of flour the cause of the strict surveillance?" I asked. "Not at all," replied the boy; "the Commissars of the mill and the soldiers know quite well where the flour goes to." I suggested that the workers might protest against such a state of affairs. "Protest, to whom?" the boy exclaimed; "we'd be called speculators and

counter-revolutionists and we'd be arrested."
"Has the Revolution given you nothing?" I
asked. "Ah, the Revolution! But that is no
more. Finished," he said bitterly.

The following morning we visited the Laferm
tobacco factory. The place was in full operation. We were conducted through the plant
and the whole process was explained to us, beginning with the sorting of the raw material and
ending with the finished cigarettes packed for
sale or shipment. The air in the workrooms
was stifling, nauseating. "The women are used
to this atmosphere," said the guide; "they don't
mind." There were some pregnant women at
work and girls no older than fourteen. They
looked haggard, their chests sunken, black rings
under their eyes. Some of them coughed and
the hectic flush of consumption showed on their
faces. "Is there a recreation room, a place
where they can eat or drink their tea and inhale
a bit of fresh air?" There was no such thing, I
was informed. The women remained at work
eight consecutive hours; they had their tea and
black bread at their benches. The system was
that of piece work, the employees receiving
twenty-five cigarettes daily above their pay
with permission to sell or exchange them.

I spoke to some of the women. They did not complain except about being compelled to live far away from the factory. In most cases it required more than two hours to go to and from work. They had asked to be quartered near the Laferm and they received a promise to that effect, but nothing more was heard of it.

Life certainly has a way of playing peculiar pranks. In America I should have scorned the idea of social welfare work: I should have considered it a cheap palliative. But in Socialist Russia the sight of pregnant women working in suffocating tobacco air and saturating themselves and their unborn with the poison impressed me as a fundamental evil. I spoke to Lisa Zorin to see whether something could not be done to ameliorate the evil. Lisa claimed that "piece work" was the only way to induce the girls to work. As to rest rooms, the women themselves had already made a fight for them, but so far nothing could be done because no space could be spared in the factory. "But if even such small improvements had not resulted from the Revolution," I argued, "what purpose has it served?" "The workers have achieved control," Lisa replied; "they are now in power, and they have more important things to attend to than rest rooms—they have the Revolution to defend." Lisa Zorin had remained very much the proletarian, but she reasoned like a nun dedicated to the service of the Church.

The thought oppressed me that what she called the "defence of the Revolution" was really only the defence of her party in power. At any rate, nothing came of my attempt at social welfare work.

CHAPTER X

THE BRITISH LABOUR MISSION

I WAS glad to learn that Angelica Balabanova arrived in Petrograd to prepare quarters for the British Labour Mission. During my stay in Moscow I had come to know and appreciate the fine spirit of Angelica. She was very devoted to me and when I fell ill she gave much time to my care, procured medicine which could be obtained only in the Kremlin drug store, and got special sick rations for me. Her friendship was generous and touching, and she endeared herself very much to me.

The Narishkin Palace was to be prepared for the Mission, and Angelica invited me to accompany her there. I noticed that she looked more worn and distressed than when I had seen her in Moscow. Our conversation made it clear to me that she suffered keenly from the reality which was so unlike her ideal. But she insisted that what seemed failure to me was conditioned in life itself, itself the greatest failure.

Narishkin Palace is situated on the southern bank of the Neva, almost opposite the Peter-and-Paul Fortress. The place was prepared for the expected guests and a number of servants and cooks installed to minister to their needs. Soon the Mission arrived—most of them typical workingmen delegates—and with them a staff of newspaper men and Mrs. Snowden. The most outstanding figure among them was Bertrand Russell, who quickly demonstrated his independence and determination to be free to investigate and learn at first hand.

In honour of the Mission the Bolsheviki organized a great demonstration on the Uritski Square. Thousands of people, among them women and children, came to show their gratitude to the English labour representatives for venturing into revolutionary Russia. The ceremony consisted of the singing of the "Internationale," followed by music and speeches, the latter translated by Balabanova in masterly fashion. Then came the military exercises. I heard Mrs. Snowden say disapprovingly, "What a display of military!" I could not resist the temptation of remarking: "Madame, remember that the big Russian army is largely the making of your own country. Had England not helped to finance the invasions into Russia, the latter could put its soldiers to useful labour."

The British Mission was entertained royally with theatres, operas, ballets, and excursions. Luxury was heaped upon them while the people slaved and went hungry. The Soviet Government left nothing undone to create a good impression and everything of a disturbing nature was kept from the visitors. Angelica hated the display and sham, and suffered keenly under the rigid watch placed upon every movement of the Mission. "Why should they not see the true state of Russia? Why should they not learn how the Russian people live?" she would lament. "Yet I am so impractical," she would correct herself; "perhaps it is all necessary." At the end of two weeks a farewell banquet was given to the visitors. Angelica insisted that I must attend. Again there were speeches and toasts, as is the custom at such functions. The speeches which seemed to ring most sincere were those of Balabanova and Madame Ravitch. The latter asked me to interpret her address, which I did. She spoke in behalf of the Russian women proletarians and praised their fortitude and devotion to the Revolution. "May the English proletarians learn the quality of their heroic Russian sisters," concluded Madame Ravitch. Mrs. Snowden, the erstwhile suffragette, had not a word in reply. She preserved a "dignified" aloofness. However, the lady became enlivened when the speeches were over and she got busy collecting autographs.

CHAPTER XI

EARLY in May two young men from the Ukraina arrived in Petrograd. Both had lived in America for a number of years and had been active in the Yiddish Labour and Anarchist movements. One of them had also been editor of an English weekly Anarchist paper, *The Alarm*, published in Chicago. In 1917, at the outbreak of the Revolution, they left for Russia together with other emigrants. Arriving in their native country, they joined the Anarchist activities there which had gained tremendous impetus through the Revolution. Their main field was the Ukraina. In 1918 they aided in the organization of the Anarchist Federation *Nabat* [Alarm], and began the publication of a paper by that name. Theoretically, they were at variance with the Bolsheviki; practically the Federation Anarchists, even as the Anarchists throughout Russia, worked with the Bolsheviki and also fought on every front against the counter-revolutionary forces.

When the two Ukrainian comrades learned of our arrival in Russia they repeatedly tried to reach us, but owing to the political conditions and the practical impossibility of travelling, they could not come north. Subsequently they had been arrested and imprisoned by the Bolsheviki. Immediately upon their release they started for Petrograd, travelling illegally. They knew the dangers confronting them— arrest and possible shooting for the possession and use of false documents—but they were willing to risk anything because they were determined that we should learn the facts about the *povstantsi* [revolutionary peasants] movements led by that extraordinary figure, Nestor Makhno. They wanted to acquaint us with the history of the Anarchist activities in Russia and relate how the iron hand of the Bolsheviki had crushed them.

During two weeks, in the stillness of the Petrograd nights, the two Ukrainian Anarchists unrolled before us the panorama of the struggle in the Ukraina. Dispassionately, quietly, and with almost uncanny detachment the young men told their story.

Thirteen different governments had "ruled" Ukraina. Each of them had robbed and murdered the peasantry, made ghastly pogroms, and left death and ruin in its way. The Ukrainian peasants, a more independent and spirited race than their northern brothers, had come to hate all governments and every measure which threatened their land and freedom. They banded together and fought back their oppressors all through the long years of the revolutionary period. The peasants had no theories; they could not be classed in any political party. Theirs was an instinctive hatred of tyranny, and practically the whole of Ukraina soon became a rebel camp. Into this seething cauldron there came, in 1917, Nestor Makhno. ✓

Makhno was a Ukrainian born. A natural rebel, he became interested in Anarchism at an early age. At seventeen he attempted the life of a Tsarist spy and was sentenced to death, but owing to his extreme youth the sentence was commuted to *katorga* for life [severe imprisonment, one third of the term in chains]. The February Revolution opened the prison doors for all political prisoners, Makhno among them. He had then spent ten years in the Butirky prison, in Moscow. He had but a limited

literature. Shortly after his liberation Makhno returned to his native village, Gulyai-Poleh, where he organized a trade union and the local soviet. Then he threw himself in the revolutionary movement and during all of 1917 he was the spiritual teacher and leader of the rebel peasants, who had risen against the landed proprietors.

In 1918, when the Brest Peace opened Ukraina to German and Austrian occupation, Makhno organized the rebel peasant bands in defence against the foreign armies. He fought against Skoropadski, the Ukrainian Hetman, who was supported by German bayonets. He waged successful guerilla warfare against Petlura, Kaledin, Grigoriev, and Denikin. A conscious Anarchist, he laboured to give the instinctive rebellion of the peasantry definite aim and purpose. It was the Makhno idea that the social revolution was to be defended against all enemies, against every counter-revolutionary or reactionary attempt from right and left. At the same time educational and cultural work was carried on among the peasants to develop them along anarchist-communist lines with the aim of establishing free peasant communes.

In February, 1919, Makhno entered into an agreement with the Red Army. He was to continue to hold the southern front against Denikin and to receive from the Bolsheviki the necessary arms and ammunition. Makhno was to remain in charge of the *povstantsi*, now grown into an army, the latter to have autonomy in its local organizations, the revolutionary soviets of the district, which covered several provinces. It was agreed that the *povstantsi* should have the right to hold conferences, freely discuss their affairs, and take action upon them. Three such conferences were held in February, March, and April. But the Bolsheviki failed to live up to the agreement. The supplies which had been promised Makhno, and which he needed desperately, would arrive after long delays or failed to come altogether. It was charged that this situation was due to the orders of Trotsky who did not look favourably upon the independent rebel army. However it be, Makhno was hampered at every step, while Denikin was gaining ground constantly. Presently the Bolsheviki began to object to the free peasant Soviets, and in

at the Makhno headquarters to settle the disputed matters. In the end the Bolshevik military representatives demanded that the *povstantsi* dissolve. The latter refused, charging the Bolsheviki with a breach of their revolutionary agreement.

Meanwhile, the Denikin advance was becoming more threatening, and Makhno still received no support from the Bolsheviki. The peasant army then decided to call a special session of the Soviet for June 15th. Definite plans and methods were to be decided upon to check the growing menace of Denikin. But on June 4th Trotsky issued an order prohibiting the holding of the Conference and declaring Makhno an outlaw. In a public meeting in Kharkov Trotsky announced that it were better to permit the Whites to remain in the Ukraina than to suffer Makhno. The presence of the Whites, he said, would influence the Ukrainian peasantry in favour of the Soviet Government, whereas Makhno and his *povstantsi* would never make peace with the Bolsheviki; they would attempt to possess themselves of some territory and to practice their ideas, which would be a constant menace to the Communist Government. It was practically a declaration of war against Makhno and his army. Soon the latter found itself attacked on two sides at once—by the Bolsheviki and Denikin. The *povstantsi* were poorly equipped and lacked the most necessary supplies for warfare, yet the peasant army for a considerable time succeeded in holding its own by the sheer military genius of its leader and the reckless courage of his devoted rebels.

At the same time the Bolsheviki began a campaign of denunciation against Makhno and his *povstantsi*. The Communist press accused him of having treacherously opened the southern front to Denikin, and branded Makhno's army a bandit gang and its leader a counterrevolutionist who must be destroyed at all cost. But this "counter-revolutionist" fully realized the Denikin menace to the Revolution. He gathered new forces and support among the peasants and in the months of September and October, 1919, his campaign against Denikin gave the latter its death blow on the Ukraina. Makhno captured Denikin's artillery base at Mariopol, annihilated the rear of the enemy's army, and succeeded in separating the main body from its base of supply. This brilliant manœuvre of Makhno and the heroic fighting of the rebel army again brought about friendly contact with the Bolsheviki. The ban was lifted from the *povstantsi* and the Communist press now began to eulogize Makhno as a great military genius and brave defender of the Revolution in the Ukraina. But the differences between Makhno and the Bolsheviki were deep-rooted: he strove to establish free peasant communes in the Ukraina, while the Communists were bent on imposing the Moscow rule. Ultimately a clash was inevitable, and it came early in January, 1920.

At that period a new enemy was threatening the Revolution. Grigoriev, formerly of the Tsarist army, later friend of the Bolsheviki, now turned against them. Having gained considerable support in the south because of his slogans of freedom and free Soviets, Grigoriev proposed to Makhno that they join forces against the Communist régime. Makhno called a meeting of the two armies and there publicly accused Grigoriev of counter-revolution and produced evidence of numerous pogroms organized by him against the Jews. Declaring Grigoriev an enemy of the people and of the Revolution,

Makhno and his staff condemned him and his aides to death, executing them on the spot. Part of Grigoriev's army joined Makhno.

Meanwhile, Denikin kept pressing Makhno, finally forcing him to withdraw from his position. Not of course without bitter fighting all along the line of nine hundred versts, the retreat lasting four months, Makhno marching toward Galicia. Denikin advanced upon Kharkov, then farther north, capturing Orel and Kursk, and finally reached the gates of Tula, in the immediate neighbourhood of Moscow.

The Red Army seemed powerless to check the advance of Denikin, but meanwhile Makhno had gathered new forces and attacked Denikin in the rear. The unexpectedness of this new turn and the extraordinary military exploits of Makhno's men in this campaign disorganized the plans of Denikin, demoralized his army, and gave the Red Army the opportunity of taking the offensive against the counter-revolutionary enemy in the neighbourhood of Tula.

When the Red Army reached Alexandrovsk, after having finally beaten the Denikin forces, Trotsky again demanded of Makhno that he disarm his men and place himself under the discipline of the Red Army. The *povstantsi* refused, whereupon an organized military campaign against the rebels was inaugurated, the Bolsheviki taking many prisoners and killing scores of others. Makhno, who managed to escape the Bolshevik net, was again declared an outlaw and bandit. Since then Makhno had been uninterruptedly waging guerilla warfare against the Bolshevik régime.

The story of the Ukrainian friends, which I have related here in very condensed form, sounded as romantic as the exploits of Stenka Rasin, the famous Cossack rebel immortalized by Gogol. Romantic and picturesque, but what bearing did the activities of Makhno and his men have upon Anarchism, I questioned the two comrades. Makhno, my informants explained, was himself an Anarchist seeking to free Ukraina from all oppression and striving to develop and organize the peasants' latent anarchistic tendencies. To this end Makhno had repeatedly called upon the Anarchists of the Ukraina and of Russia to aid him. He offered them the widest opportunity for propagandistic and educational work, supplied them with printing outfits and meeting places, and gave them the fullest liberty of action. Whenever Makhno captured a city, freedom of speech and press for Anarch-

ists and Left Social Revolutionists was established. Makhno often said: "I am a military
man and I have no time for educational work.
But you who are writers and speakers, you can
do that work. Join me and together we shall be
able to prepare the field for a real Anarchist
experiment." But the chief value of the Makhno movement lay in the peasants themselves,
my comrades thought. It was a spontaneous,
elemental movement, the peasants' opposition
to all governments being the result not of
theories but of bitter experience and of instinctive love of liberty. They were fertile ground for
Anarchist ideas. For this reason a number of
Anarchists joined Makhno. They were with
him in most of his military campaigns and
energetically carried on Anarchist propaganda
during that time.

I have been told by Zorin and other Communists that Makhno was a Jew-baiter and that his
povstantsi were responsible for numerous brutal
pogroms. My visitors emphatically denied the
charges. Makhno bitterly fought pogroms, they
stated; he had often issued proclamations against
such outrages, and he had even with his own
hand punished some of those guilty of assault
on Jews. Hatred of the Hebrew was of course

even among the Red soldiers. They, too, have assaulted, robbed, and outraged Jews; yet no one holds the Bolsheviki responsible for such isolated instances. The Ukraina is infested with armed bands who are often mistaken for Makhnovtsi and who have made pogroms. The Bolsheviki, aware of this, have exploited the confusion to discredit Makhno and his followers. However, the Anarchist of the Ukraina—I was informed— did not idealize the Makhno movement. They knew that the *povstantsi* were not conscious Anarchists. Their paper *Nabat* had repeatedly emphasized this fact. On the other hand, the Anarchists could not overlook the importance of popular movement which was instinctively rebellious, anarchistically inclined, and successful in driving back the enemies of the Revolution, which the better organized and equipped Bolshevik army could not accomplish. For this reason many Anarchists considered it their duty to work with Makhno. But the bulk remained away; they had their larger cultural, educational, and organizing work to do.

The invading counter-revolutionary forces, though differing in character and purpose, all agreed in their relentless persecution of the

Anarchists. The latter were made to suffer, whatever the new régime. The Bolsheviki were no better in this regard than Denikin or any other White element. Anarchists filled Bolshevik prisons; many had been shot and all legal Anarchist activities were suppressed. The Tcheka especially was doing ghastly work, having resurrected the old Tsarist methods, including even torture.

My young visitors spoke from experience: they had repeatedly been in Bolshevik prisons themselves.

CHAPTER XII

BENEATH THE SURFACE

THE terrible story I had been listening to for two weeks broke over me like a storm. Was this the Revolution I had believed in all my life, yearned for, and strove to interest others in, or was it a caricature—a hideous monster that had come to jeer and mock me? The Communists I had met daily during six months—self-sacrificing, hard-working men and women imbued with a high ideal—were such people capable of the treachery and horrors charged against them? Zinoviev, Radek, Zorin, Ravitch, and many others I had learned to know—could they in the name of an ideal lie, defame, torture, kill? But, then—had not Zorin told me that capital punishment had been abolished in Russia? Yet I learned shortly after my arrival that hundreds of people had been shot on the very eve of the day when the new decree went into effect, and that as a matter of fact shooting by the Tcheka had never ceased.

That my friends were not exaggerating when they spoke of tortures by the Tcheka, I also learned from other sources. Complaints about the fearful conditions in Petrograd prisons had become so numerous that Moscow was apprised of the situation. A Tcheka inspector came to investigate. The prisoners being afraid to speak, immunity was promised them. But no sooner had the inspector left than one of the inmates, a young boy, who had been very outspoken about the brutalities practised by the Tcheka, was dragged out of his cell and cruelly beaten.

Why did Zorin resort to lies? Surely he must have known that I would not remain in the dark very long. And then, was not Lenin also guilty of the same methods? "Anarchists of ideas [*ideyni*] are not in our prisons," he had assured me. Yet at that very moment numerous Anarchists filled the jails of Moscow and Petrograd and of many other cities in Russia. In May, 1920, scores of them had been arrested in Petrograd, among them two girls of seventeen and nineteen years of age. None of the prisoners were charged with counter-revolutionary activities: they were "Anarchists of ideas," to use Lenin's expression. Several of them had issued a manifesto for the First of May, calling attention to the appalling conditions in the factories of the Socialist Republic. The two young girls who had circulated a handbill against the "labour book," which had then just gone into effect, were also arrested.

The labour book was heralded by the Bolsheviki as one of the great Communist achievements. It would establish equality and abolish parasitism, it was claimed. As a matter of fact, the labour book was somewhat of the character of the yellow ticket issued to prostitutes under the Tsarist régime. It was a record of every step one made, and without it no step could be made. It bound its holder to his job, to the city he lived in, and to the room he occupied. It recorded one's political faith and party adherence, and the number of times he was arrested. In short, a yellow ticket. Even some Communists resented the degrading innovation. The Anarchists who protested against it were arrested by the Tcheka. When certain leading Communists were approached in the matter they repeated what Lenin had said: "No Anarchists of ideas are in our prisons."

The aureole was falling from the Communists. All of them seemed to believe that the end justified the means. I recalled the statements of

Radek at the first anniversary of the Third International, when he related to his audience the "marvellous spread of Communism" in America "Fifty thousand Communists are in American prisons," he exclaimed. "Molly Stimer, a girl of eighteen, and her male companions, all Communists, had been deported from America for their Communist activities." I thought at the time that Radek was misinformed. Yet it seemed strange that he did not make sure of his facts before making such assertions. They were dishonest and an insult to Molly Stimer and her Anarchist comrades, added to the injustice they had suffered at the hands of the American plutocracy.

During the past several months I had seen and heard enough to become somewhat conversant with the Communist psychology, as well as with the theories and methods of the Bolsheviki. I was no longer surprised at the story of their double-dealing with Makhno, the brutalities practised by the Tcheka, the lies of Zorin. I had come to realize that the Communists believed implicitly in the Jesuitic formula that the end justifies *all* means. In fact, they gloried in that formula. Any suggestion

Bolsheviki the end to be achieved was the Communist State, or the so-called Dictatorship of the Proletariat. Everything which advanced that end was justifiable and revolutionary. The Lenins, Radeks, and Zorins were therefore quite consistent. Obsessed by the infallibility of their creed, giving of themselves to the fullest, they could be both heroic and despicable at the same time. They could work twenty hours a day, live on herring and tea, and order the slaughter of innocent men and women. Occasionally they sought to mask their killings by pretending a "misunderstanding," for doesn't the end justify all means? They could employ torture and deny the inquisition, they could lie and defame, and call themselves idealists. In short, they could make themselves and others believe that everything was legitimate and right from the revolutionary viewpoint; any other policy was weak, sentimental, or a betrayal of the Revolution.

On a certain occasion, when I passed criticism on the brutal way delicate women were driven into the streets to shovel snow, insisting that even if they had belonged to the bourgeoisie they were human, and that physical fitness should be taken into consideration, a Communist said to me: "You should be ashamed of yourself; you, an old revolutionist, and yet so sentimental." It was the same attitude that some Communists assumed toward Angelica Balabanova, because she was always solicitous and eager to help wherever possible. In short, I had come to see that the Bolsheviki were social puritans who sincerely believed that they alone were ordained to save mankind. My relations with the Bolsheviki became more strained, my attitude toward the Revolution as I found it more critical.

One thing grew quite clear to me: I could not affiliate myself with the Soviet Government; I could not accept any work which would place me under the control of the Communist machine. The Commissariat of Education was so thoroughly dominated by that machine that it was hopeless to expect anything but routine work. In fact, unless one was a Communist one could accomplish almost nothing. I had been eager to join Lunacharsky, whom I considered one of the most cultivated and least dogmatic of the

Communists in high position. But I became convinced that Lunacharsky himself was a helpless cog in the machine, his best efforts constantly curtailed and checked. I had also learned a great deal about the system of favouritism and graft that prevailed in the management of the schools and the treatment of children. Some schools were in splendid condition, the children well fed and well clad, enjoying concerts, theatricals, dances, and other amusements. But the majority of the schools and children's homes were squalid, dirty, and neglected. Those in charge of the "preferred" schools had little difficulty in procuring everything needed for their charges, often having an over-supply. But the caretakers of the "common" schools would waste their time and energies by the week going about from one department to another, discouraged and faint with endless waiting before they could obtain the merest necessities.

At first I ascribed this condition of affairs to the scarcity of food and materials. I heard it said often enough that the blockade and intervention were responsible. To a large extent that was true. Had Russia not been so starved, mismanagement and graft would not have had such fatal results. But added to the prevalent scarcity of things was the dominant notion of Communist propaganda. Even the children had to serve that end. The well-kept schools were for show, for the foreign missions and delegates who were visiting Russia. Everything was lavished on these show schools at the cost of the others.

I remembered how everybody was startled in Petrograd by an article in the Petrograd *Pravda* of May, disclosing appalling conditions in the schools. A committee of the Young Communist organizations investigated some of the institutions. They found the children dirty, full of vermin, sleeping on filthy mattresses, fed on miserable food, punished by being locked in dark rooms for the night, forced to go without their suppers, and even beaten. The number of officials and employees in the schools was nothing less than criminal. In one school, for instance, there were 138 of them to 125 children. In another, 40 to 25 children. All these parasites were taking the bread from the very mouths of the unfortunate children.

The Zorins had spoken to me repeatedly of Lillina, the woman in charge of the Petrograd Educational Department. She was a wonderful

impressed: she looked prim and self-satisfied, a typical Puritan schoolma'am. But I would not form an opinion until I had talked with her. At the publication of the school disclosures I decided to see Lillina. We conversed over an hour about the schools in her charge, about education in general, the problem of defective children and their treatment. She made light of the abuses in her schools, claiming that "the young comrades had exaggerated the defects." At any rate, she added, the guilty had already been removed from the schools.

Similarly to many other responsible Communists Lillina was consecrated to her work and gave all her time and energies to it. Naturally, she could not personally oversee everything; the show schools being the most important in her estimation, she devoted most of her time to them. The other schools were left in the care of her numerous assistants, whose fitness for the work was judged largely according to their political usefulness. Our talk strengthened my conviction that I could have no part in the work of the Bolshevik Board of Education.

The Board of Health offered as little opportunity for real service—service that should not discriminate in favour of show hospitals or the political views of the patients. This principle of discrimination prevailed, unfortunately, even in the sick rooms. Like all Communist institutions, the Board of Health was headed by a political Commissar, Doctor Pervukhin. He was anxious to secure my assistance, proposing to put me in charge of factory, dispensary, or district nursing—a very flattering and tempting offer, and one that appealed to me strongly. I had several conferences with Doctor Pervukhin, but they led to no practical result.

Whenever I visited his department I found groups of men and women waiting, endlessly waiting. They were doctors and nurses, members of the *intelligentsia*—none of them Communists—who were employed in various medical branches, but their time and energies were being wasted in the waiting rooms of Doctor Pervukhin, the political Commissar. They were a sorry lot, dispirited and dejected, those men and women, once the flower of Russia. Was I to join this tragic procession, submit to the political yoke? Not until I should become convinced that the yoke was indispensable to the revolutionary process would I consent to it. I felt that

I must first secure work of a non-partisan character, work that would enable me to study conditions in Russia and get into direct touch with the people, the workers and peasants. Only then should I be able to find my way out of the chaos of doubt and mental anguish that I had fallen prey to.

CHAPTER XIII

JOINING THE MUSEUM OF THE REVOLUTION

THE Museum of the Revolution is housed in the Winter Palace, in the suite once used as the nursery of the Tsar's children. The entrance to that part of the palace is known as *detsky podyezd.* From the windows of the palace the Tsar must have often looked across the Neva at the Peter-and-Paul Fortress, the living tomb of his political enemies. How different things were now! The thought of it kindled my imagination. I was full of the wonder and the magic of the great change when I paid my first visit to the Museum.

I found groups of men and women at work in the various rooms, huddled up in their wraps and shivering with cold. Their faces were bloated and bluish, their hands frost-bitten, their whole appearance shadow-like. What must be the devotion of these people, I thought, when they can continue to work under such conditions. The secretary of the Museum, M. B. Kaplan received me very cordially and expressed "the hope that I would join in the work of the Museum." He and another member of the staff spent considerable time with me on several occasions, explaining the plans and purposes of the Museum. They asked me to join the expedition which the Museum was then organizing, and which was to go south to the Ukraina and the Caucasus. Valuable material of the revolutionary period was to be gathered there, they explained. The idea attracted me. Aside from my general interest in the Museum and its efforts, it meant non-partisan work, free from Commissars, and an exceptional opportunity to see and study Russia.

In the course of our acquaintance I learned that neither Mr. Kaplan nor his friend was a Communist. But while Mr. Kaplan was strongly pro-Bolshevik and tried to defend and explain away everything, the other man was critical though by no means antagonistic. During my stay in Petrograd I saw much of both men, and I learned from them a great deal about the Revolution and the methods of the Bolsheviki. Kaplan's friend, whose name for obvious reasons I cannot mention, often spoke of the utter impossibility of doing creative work within the Communist machine. "The Bolsheviki," he would say, "always complain about lack of able help, yet no one—unless a Communist—has much of a chance." The Museum was among the least interfered with institutions, and work there had been progressing well. Then a group of twenty youths were sent over, young and inexperienced boys unfamiliar with the work. Being Communists they were placed in positions of authority, and friction and confusion resulted. Everyone felt himself watched and spied upon. "The Bolsheviki care not about merit," he said; "their chief concern is a membership card." He was not enthusiastic about the future of the Museum, yet believed that the coöperation of the "Americans" would aid its proper development.

Finally I decided on the Museum as offering the most suitable work for me, mainly because that institution was non-partisan. I had hoped for a more vital share in Russia's life than the collecting of historical material; still I considered it valuable and necessary work. When I had definitely consented to become a member of the expedition, I visited the Museum daily to help with the preparations for the long journey. There was much work. It was no easy matter to obtain a car, equip it for the arduous trip,

and secure the documents which would give us access to the material we set out to collect.

While I was busy aiding in these preparations Angelica Balabanova arrived in Petrograd to meet the Italian Mission. She seemed transformed. She had longed for her Italian comrades: they would bring her a breath of her beloved Italy, of her former life and work there. Though Russian by birth, training, and revolutionary traditions, Angelica had become rooted in the soil of Italy. Well I understood her and her sense of strangeness in the country, the hard soil of which was to bear a new and radiant life. Angelica would not admit even to herself that the much hoped-for life was stillborn. But knowing her as I did, it was not difficult for me to understand how bitter was her grief over the hapless and formless thing that had come to Russia. But now her beloved Italians were coming! They would bring with them the warmth and colour of Italy.

The Italians came and with them new festivities, demonstrations, meetings, and speeches. How different it all appeared to me from my memorable first days on Belo-Ostrov. No doubt the Italians now felt as awed as I did then, as inspired by the seeming wonder of Russia. Six months and the close proximity with the reality of things quite changed the picture for me. The spontaneity, the enthusiasm, the vitality had all gone out of it. Only a pale shadow remained, a grinning phantom that clutched at my heart.

On the Uritski Square the masses were growing weary with long waiting. They had been kept there for hours before the Italian Mission arrived from the Tauride Palace. The ceremonies were just beginning when a woman leaning against the platform, wan and pale, began to weep. I stood close by. "It is easy for them to talk," she moaned, "but we've had no food all day. We received orders to march directly from our work on pain of losing our bread rations. Since five this morning I am on my feet. We were not permitted to go home after work to our bit of dinner. We had to come here. Seventeen hours on a piece of bread and some *kipyatok* [boiled water]. Do the visitors know anything about us?" The speeches went on, the "Internationale" was being repeated for the tenth time, the sailors performed their fancy exercises and the claqueurs on the reviewing stand were shouting hurrahs. I rushed away. I, too, was weeping, though my eyes remained dry.

The Italian, like the English, Mission was

quartered in the Narishkin Palace. One day, on visiting Angelica there, I found her in a perturbed state of mind. Through one of the servants she had learned that the ex-princess Narishkin, former owner of the palace, had come to beg for the silver ikon which had been in the family for generations. "Just that ikon," she had implored. But the ikon was now state property, and Balabanova could do nothing about it. "Just think," Angelica said, "Narishkin, old and desolate, now stands on the street corner begging, and I live in this palace. How dreadful is life! I am no good for it; I must get away."

But Angelica was bound by party discipline; she stayed on in the palace until she returned to Moscow. I know she did not feel much happier than the ragged and starving ex-princess begging on the street corner.

Balabanova, anxious that I should find suitable work, informed me one day that Petrovsky, known in America as Doctor Goldfarb, had arrived in Petrograd. He was Chief of the Central Military Education Department, which included Nurses' Training Schools. I had never met the man in the States, but I had heard of him as the labour editor of the New York *For-*

ward, the Jewish Socialist daily. He offered me the position of head instructress in the military Nurses' Training School, with a view to introducing American methods of nursing, or to send me with a medical train to the Polish front. I had proffered my services at the first news of the Polish attack on Russia: I felt the Revolution in danger, and I hastened to Zorin to ask to be assigned as a nurse. He promised to bring the matter before the proper authorities, but I heard nothing further about it. I was, therefore, somewhat surprised at the proposition of Petrovsky. However, it came too late. What I had since learned about the situation in the Ukraina, the Bolshevik methods toward Makhno and the *povstantsi* movement, the persecution of Anarchists, and the Tcheka activities, had completely shaken my faith in the Bolsheviki as revolutionists. The offer came too late. But Moscow perhaps thought it unwise to let me see behind the scenes at the front; Petrovsky failed to inform me of the Moscow decision. I felt relieved.

At last we received the glad tidings that the greatest difficulty had been overcome: a car for the Museum Expedition had been secured. It consisted of six compartments and was newly painted and cleaned. Now began the work of equipment. Ordinarily it would have taken another two months, but we had the co-operation of the man at the head of the Museum, Chairman Yatmanov, a Communist. He was also in charge of all the properties of the Winter Palace where the Museum is housed. The largest part of the linen, silver, and glassware from the Tsar's storerooms had been removed, but there was still much left. Supplied with an order of the chairman I was shown over what was once guarded as sacred precincts by Romanov flunkeys. I found rooms stacked to the ceiling with rare and beautiful china and compartments filled with the finest linen. The basement, running the whole length of the Winter Palace, was stocked with kitchen utensils of every size and variety. Tin plates and pots would have been more appropriate for the Expedition, but owing to the ruling that no institution may draw upon another for anything it has in its own possession, there was nothing to do but to choose the simplest obtainable at the Winter Palace. I went home reflecting upon the strangeness of life: revolutionists eating out of the crested service of the Romanovs. But I felt no elation over it.

CHAPTER XIV

PETROPAVLOVSK AND SCHLÜSSELBURG

AS SOME time was to pass before we could depart, I took advantage of the opportunity which presented itself to visit the historic prisons, the Peter-and-Paul Fortress and Schlüsselburg. I recollected the dread and awe the very names of these places filled me with when I first came to Petrograd as a child of thirteen. In fact, my dread of the Petropavlovsk Fortress dated back to a much earlier time. I think I must have been six years old when a great shock had come to our family: we learned that my mother's oldest brother, Yegor, a student at the University of Petersburg, had been arrested and was held in the Fortress. My mother at once set out for the capital. We children remained at home in fear and trepidation lest Mother should not find our uncle among the living. We spent anxious weeks and months till finally Mother returned. Great was our rejoicing to hear that she had rescued her brother

shock remained with me for a long time.

Seven years later, my family then living in Petersburg, I happened to be sent on an errand which took me past the Peter-and-Paul Fortress. The shock I had received many years before revived within me with paralyzing force. There stood the heavy mass of stone, dark and sinister. I was terrified. The great prison was still to me a haunted house, causing my heart to palpitate with fear whenever I had to pass it. Years later, when I had begun to draw sustenance from the lives and heroism of the great Russian revolutionists, the Peter-and-Paul Fortress became still more hateful. And now I was about to enter its mysterious walls and see with my own eyes the place which had been the living grave of so many of the best sons and daughters of Russia.

The guide assigned to take us through the different ravelins had been in the prison for ten years. He knew every stone in the place. But the silence told me more than all the information of the guide. The martyrs who had beaten their wings against the cold stone, striving upward toward the light and air, came to life for me. The Dekabristi, Tchernishevsky, Dostoy-

spoke in a thousand-throated voice of their social idealism and their personal suffering—of their high hopes and fervent faith in the ultimate liberation of Russia. Now the fluttering spirits of the heroic dead may rest in peace: their dream has come true. But what is this strange writing on the wall? "To-night I am to be shot because I had once acquired an education." I had almost lost consciousness of the reality. The inscription roused me to it. "What is this?" I asked the guard. "Those are the last words of an *intelligent*," he replied. "After the October Revolution the *intelligentsia* filled this prison. From here they were taken out and shot, or were loaded on barges never to return. Those were dreadful days and still more dreadful nights " So the dream of those who had given their lives for the liberation of Russia had not come true, after all. Is there any change in the world? Or is it all an eternal recurrence of man's inhumanity to man?

We reached the strip of enclosure where the prisoners used to be permitted a half-hour's recreation. One by one they had to walk up and down the narrow lane in dead silence, with the sentries on the wall ready to shoot for the slightest infraction of the rules. And while the caged and fettered ones treaded the treeless walk, the all-powerful Romanovs looked out of the Winter Palace toward the golden spire topping the Fortress to reassure themselves that their hated enemies would never again threaten their safety. But not even Petropavlovsk could save the Tsars from the slaying hand of Time and Revolution. Indeed, there *is* change; slow and painful, but come it does.

In the enclosure we met Angelica Balabanova and the Italians. We walked about the huge prison, each absorbed in his own thoughts set in motion by what he saw. Would Angelica notice the writing on the wall, I wondered. "To-night I am to be shot because I had once acquired an education."

Some time later several of our group made a trip to Schlüsselburg, the even more dreadful tomb of the political enemies of Tsarism. It is a journey of several hours by boat up the beautiful River Neva. The day was chilly and gray, as was our mood; just the right state of mind to visit Schlüsselburg. The fortress was strongly guarded, but our Museum permit secured for us immediate admission. Schlüsselburg is a compact mass of stone perched upon a high rock in

the open sea. For many decades only the victims of court intrigues and royal disfavour were
immured within its impenetrable walls, but
later it became the Golgotha of the political
enemies of the Tsarist régime.

I had heard of Schlüsselburg when my parents
first came to Petersburg; but unlike my feeling
toward the Peter-and-Paul Fortress, I had no
personal reaction to the place. It was Russian
revolutionary literature which brought the meaning of Schlüsselburg home to me. Especially the
story of Volkenstein, one of the two women who
had spent long years in the dreaded place, left an
indelible impression on my mind. Yet nothing
I had read made the place quite so real and terri-
fying as when I climbed up the stone steps and
stood before the forbidding gates. As far as
any effect upon the physical condition of the
Peter-and-Paul Fortress was concerned, the
Revolution might never have taken place. The
prison remained intact, ready for immediate
use by the new régime. Not so Schlüsselburg.
The wrath of the proletariat struck that house
of the dead almost to the ground.

How cruel and perverse the human mind
which could create a Schlüsselburg! Verily, no
savage could be guilty of the fiendish spirit that

conceived this appalling tomb. Cells built like a bag, without doors or windows and with only a small opening through which the victims were lowered into their living grave. Other cells were stone cages to drive the mind to madness and lacerate the heart of the unfortunates. Yet men and women endured twenty years in this terrible place. What fortitude, what power of endurance, what sublime faith one must have had to hold out, to emerge from it alive! Here Netchaev, Lopatin, Morosov, Volkenstein, Figner, and others of the splendid band spent their tortured lives. Here is the common grave of Ulianov, Mishkin, Kalayev, Balmashev, and many more. The black tablet inscribed with their names speaks louder than the voices silenced for ever. Not even the roaring waves dashing against the rock of Schlüsselburg can drown that accusing voice.

Petropavlovsk and Schlüsselburg stand as the living proof of how futile is the hope of the mighty to escape the Frankensteins of their own making.

CHAPTER XV

THE TRADE UNIONS

IT WAS the month of June and the time of our departure was approaching. Petrograd seemed more beautiful than ever; the white nights had come—almost broad daylight without its glare, the mysterious soothing white nights of Petrograd. There were rumours of counter-revolutionary danger and the city was guarded against attack. Martial law prevailing, it was forbidden to be out on the streets after 1 A. M., even though it was almost daylight. Occasionally special permits were obtained by friends and then we would walk through the deserted streets or along the banks of the dark Neva, discussing in whispers the perplexing situation. I sought for some outstanding feature in the blurred picture—the Russian Revolution, a huge flame shooting across the world illuminating the black horizon of the disinherited and oppressed—the Revolution, the new hope, the great spiritual awakening. And here I was in the midst of it, yet nowhere could I see the promise and fulfilment of the great event. Had I misunderstood the meaning and nature of revolution? Perhaps the wrong and the evil I have seen during those five months were inseparable from a revolution. Or was it the political machine which the Bolsheviki have created—is that the force which is crushing the Revolution? If I had witnessed the birth of the latter I should now be better able to judge. But apparently I arrived at the end—the agonizing end of a people. It is all so complex, so impenetrable, a *tupik*, a blind alley, as the Russians call it. Only time and earnest study, aided by sympathetic understanding, will show me the way out. Meanwhile, I must keep up my courage and —away from Petrograd, out among the people.

Presently the long-awaited moment arrived. On June 30, 1920, our car was coupled to a slow train called "Maxim Gorki," and we pulled out of the Nikolayevski station, bound for Moscow.

In Moscow there were many formalities to go through with. We thought a few days would suffice, but we remained two weeks. However, our stay was interesting. The city was alive with delegates to the Second Congress of the Third International; from all parts of the world the workers had sent their comrades to the promised land, revolutionary Russia, the first republic of the workers. Among the delegates there were also Anarchists and syndicalists who believed as firmly as I did six months previously that the Bolsheviki were the symbol of the Revolution. They had responded to the Moscow call with enthusiasm. Some of them I had met in Petrograd and now they were eager to hear of my experiences and learn my opinions. But what was I to tell them, and would they believe me if I did? Would I have believed any adverse criticism before I came to Russia? Besides, I felt that my views regarding the Bolsheviki were still too unformed, too vague, a conglomeration of mere impressions. My old values had been shattered and so far I have been unable to replace them. I could therefore not speak on the fundamental questions, but I did inform my friends that the Moscow and Petrograd prisons were crowded with Anarchists and other revolutionists, and I advised them not to content themselves with the official explanations but to investigate for themselves. I warned them that they would be surrounded by guides and interpreters, most of them men of the Tcheka, and that they would not be able to learn the facts unless they made a determined, independent effort.

at the time. The Printers' Union had been suppressed and its entire managing board sent to prison. The Union had called a public meet ing to which members of the British Labour Mission were invited. There the famous Social ist Revolutionist Tchernov had unexpectedly made his appearance. He severely criticised the Bolshevik régime, received an ovation from the huge audience of workers, and then vanished as mysteriously as he had come. The Menshevik Dan was less successful. He also addressed the meeting, but he failed to make his escape: he landed in the Tcheka. The next morning the Moscow *Pravda* and the *Izvestia* denounced the action of the Printers' Union as counter-revolutionary, and raged about Tchernov having been permitted to speak. The papers called for exemplary punishment of the printers who dared defy the Soviet Government.

The Bakers' Union, a very militant organiza-tion, had also been suppressed, and its manage-ment replaced by Communists. Several months before, in March, I had attended a convention of the bakers. The delegates impressed me as a courageous group who did not fear to criticise the Bolshevik régime and present the demands of the workers. I wondered then that they were permitted to continue the conference, for they were outspoken in their opposition to the Communists. "The bakers are 'Shkurniki' [skinners]," I was told; "they always instigate strikes, and only counter-revolutionists can wish to strike in the workers' Republic." But it seemed to me that the workers could not follow such reasoning. They did strike. They even committed a more heinous crime: they refused to vote for the Communist candidate, electing instead a man of their own choice. This action of the bakers was followed by the arrest of several of their more active members. Naturally the workers resented the arbitrary methods of the Government.

Later I met some of the bakers and found them much embittered against the Communist Party and the Government. I inquired about the condition of their union, telling them that I had been informed that the Russian unions were very powerful and had practical control of the industrial life of the country. The bakers laughed. "The trade unions are the lackeys of the Government," they said; "they have no independent function, and the workers have no say in them. The trade unions are doing mere police duty for the Government.") That sounded quite different from the story told by Melnichansky, the chairman of the Moscow Trade Union Soviet, whom I had met on my first visit to Moscow.

On that occasion he had shown me about the trade union headquarters known as the *Dom Soyusov*, and explained how the organization worked. Seven million workers were in the trade unions, he said; all trades and professions belonged to it. The workers themselves managed the industries and owned them. "The building you are in now is also owned by the unions," he remarked with pride; "formerly it was the House of the Nobility." The room we were in had been used for festive assemblies and the great nobles sat in crested chairs around the table in the centre. Melnichansky showed me the secret underground passage hidden by a little turntable, through which the nobles could escape in case of danger. They never dreamed that the workers would some day gather around the same table and sit in the beautiful hall of marble columns. The educational and cultural work done by the trade unions, the chairman further explained, was of the greatest scope. "We have our workers' colleges and other cultural institutions giving courses and lectures on various subjects. They are all managed by the workers. The unions own their own means of recreation, and we have access to all the theatres." It was apparent from his explanation that the trade unions of Russia had reached a point far beyond anything known by labour organizations in Europe and America.

A similar account I had heard from Tsiperovitch, the chairman of the Petrograd trade unions, with whom I had made my first trip to Moscow. He had also shown me about the Petrograd Labour Temple, a beautiful and spacious building where the Petrograd unions had their offices. His recital also made it clear that the workers of Russia had at last come into their own.

But gradually I began to see the other side of the medal. I found that like most things in Russia the trade union picture had a double facet: one paraded before foreign visitors and "investigators," the other known by the masses. The bakers and the printers had recently been shown the other side. It was a lesson of the benefits that accrued to the trade unions in the Socialist Republic.

In March I had attended an election meeting

cow factories. It was the most exciting gathering I had witnessed in Russia—the dimly lit hall in the factory club rooms, the faces of the men and women worn with privation and suffering, the intense feeling over the wrong done them, all impressed me very strongly. Their chosen representative, an Anarchist, had been refused his mandate by the Soviet authorities. It was the third time the workers gathered to re-elect their delegate to the Moscow Soviet, and every time they elected the same man. The Communist candidate opposing him was Semashko, the Commissar of the Department of Health. I had expected to find an educated and cultured man. But the behaviour and language of the Commissar at that election meeting would have put a hod-carrier to shame. He raved against the workers for choosing a non-Communist, called anathema upon their heads, and threatened them with the Tcheka and the curtailment of their rations. But he had no effect upon the audience except to emphasize their opposition to him, and to arouse antagonism against the party he represented. The final victory, however, was with Semashko. The workers' choice was repudiated by the authorities and later even arrested and imprisoned. That was in March. In May, during the visit of the British Labour Mission, the factory candidate together with other political prisoners declared a hunger strike which resulted in their liberation.

The story told me by the bakers of their election experiences had the quality of our own Wild West during its pioneer days. Tchekists with loaded guns were in the habit of attending gatherings of the unions and they made it clear what would happen if the workers should fail to elect a Communist. But the bakers, a strong and militant organization, would not be intimidated. They declared that no bread would be baked in Moscow unless they were permitted to elect their own candidate. That had the desired effect. After the meeting the Tchekists tried to arrest the candidate-elect, but the bakers surrounded him and saw him safely home. The next day they sent their ultimatum to the authorities, demanding recognition of their choice and threatening to strike in case of refusal. Thus the bakers triumphed and gained an advantage over their less courageous brothers in the other labour organizations of minor importance. In starving Russia the work of the bakers was as vital as life itself.

CHAPTER XVI

MARIA SPIRIDONOVA

THE Commissariat of Education also included the Department of Museums. The Petrograd Museum of the Revolution had two chairmen; Lunacharsky being one of them, it was necessary to secure his signature to our credentials which had already been signed by Zinoviev, the second chairman of the Museum. I was commissioned to see Lunacharsky.

I felt rather guilty before him. I left Moscow in March promising to return within a week to join him in his work. Now, four months later, I came to ask his coöperation in an entirely different field. I went to the Kremlin determined to tell Lunacharsky how I felt about the situation in Russia. But I was relieved of the necessity by the presence of a number of people in his office; there was no time to take the matter up. I could merely inform Lunacharsky of the purpose of the expedition and request his aid in the work. It met with his approval. He signed our credentials and also supplied me with letters of introduction and recommendation to facilitate our efforts in behalf of the Museum.

While our Commission was making the necessary preparations for the trip to the Ukraine, I found time to visit various institutions in Moscow and to meet some interesting people. Among them were certain well-known Left Social Revolutionists whom I had met on my previous visit. I had told them then that I was eager to visit Maria Spiridonova, of whose condition I had heard many conflicting stories. But at that time no meeting could be arranged: it might have exposed Spiridonova to danger, for she was living illegally, as a peasant woman. History indeed repeats itself. Under the Tsar Spiridonova, also disguised as a country girl, had shaddowed Lukhanovsky, the Governor of Tamboy, of peasant-flogging fame. Having shot him, she was arrested, tortured, and later sentenced to death. The western world became aroused, and it was due to its protests that the sentence of Spiridonova was changed to Siberian exile for life. She spent eleven years there; the February Revolution brought her freedom and back to Russia. Maria Spiridonova immediately threw herself into revolutionary activity. Now, in the Socialist Republic, Maria was again living in disguise after having escaped from the prison in the Kremlin.

Arrangements were finally made to enable me to visit Spiridonova, and I was cautioned to make sure that I was not followed by Tcheka men. We agreed with Maria's friends upon a meeting place and from there we zigzagged a number of streets till we at last reached the top floor of a house in the back of a yard. I was led into a small room containing a bed, small desk, bookcase, and several chairs. Before the desk, piled high with letters and papers, sat a frail little woman, Maria Spiridonova. This, then, was one of Russia's great martyrs, this woman who had so unflinchingly suffered the tortures inflicted upon her by the Tsar's henchmen. I had been told by Zorin and Jack Reed that Spiridonova had suffered a breakdown, and was kept in a sanatorium. Her malady, they said, was acute neurasthenia and hysteria. When I came face to face with Maria, I immediately realized that both men had deceived me. I was no longer surprised at Zorin: much of what he had told me I gradually discovered to be utterly false. As to Reed, unfamiliar with the language and completely under the sway of the new faith, he took too much for granted. Thus, on his return from Moscow he came to inform me that the story of the shooting of prisoners *en masse* on the eve of the abolition of capital punishment was really true; but, he assured me, it was all the fault of a certain official of the Tcheka who had already paid with his life for it. I had opportunity to investigate the matter. I found that Jack had again been misled. It was not that a certain man was responsible for the wholesale killing on that occasion. The act was conditioned in the whole system and character of the Tcheka.

I spent two days with Maria Spiridonova, listening to her recital of events since October, 1917. She spoke at length about the enthusiasm and zeal of the masses and the hopes held out by the Bolsheviki; of their ascendancy to power and gradual turn to the right. She explained the Brest-Litovsk peace which she considered as the first link in the chain that has since fettered the Revolution. She dwelt on the *razverstka*, the system of forcible requisition, which was devastating Russia and discrediting everything the Revolution had been fought for; she referred to the terrorism practised by the Bolsheviki against every revolutionary criticism, to the new Communist bureaucracy and inefficiency, and the hopelessness of the whole situation. It was a crushing indictment against the Bolsheviki, their theories and methods.

If Spiridonova had really suffered a breakdown, as I had been assured, and was hysterical and mentally unbalanced, she must have had extraordinary control of herself. She was calm, self-contained, and clear on every point. She had the fullest command of her material and information. On several occasions during her narrative, when she detected doubt in my face, she remarked: "I fear you don't quite believe me. Well, here is what some of the peasants write me," and she would reach over to a pile of letters on her desk and read to me passages heart-rending with misery and bitter against the Bolsheviki. In stilted handwriting, sometimes almost illegible, the peasants of the Ukraine and Siberia wrote of the horrors of the *razverstka* and what it had done to them and their land. "They have taken away everything, even the last seeds for the next sowing." "The Commissars have robbed us of everything." Thus ran the letters. Frequently peasants wanted to know whether Spiridonova had gone over to the Bolsheviki. "If you also forsake us, *ma-*

tushka, we have no one to turn to," one peasant wrote.

The enormity of her accusations challenged credence. After all, the Bolsheviki were revolutionists. How could they be guilty of the terrible things charged against them? Perhaps they were not responsible for the situation as it had developed; they had the whole world against them. There was the Brest peace, for instance. When the news of it first reached America I happened to be in prison. I reflected long and carefully whether Soviet Russia was justified in negotiating with German imperialism. But I could see no way out of the situation. I was in favour of the Brest peace. Since I came to Russia I heard conflicting versions of it. Nearly everyone, excepting the Communists, considered the Brest agreement as much a betrayal of the Revolution as the rôle of the German Socialists in the war—a betrayal of the spirit of interna tionalism. The Communists, on the other hand, were unanimous in defending the peace and denouncing as counter-revolutionist everybody who questioned the wisdom and the revolutionary justification of that agreement. "We could do nothing else," argued the Communists. "Germany had a mighty army, while we had none. Had we refused to sign the Brest treaty we should have sealed the fate of the Revolution. We realized that Brest meant a compromise, but we knew that the workers of Russia and the rest of the world would understand that we had been forced to it. Our compromise was similar to that of workers when they are forced to accept the conditions of their masters after an unsuccessful strike."

But Spiridonova was not convinced. "There is not one word of truth in the argument advanced by the Bolsheviki," she said. It is true that Russia had no disciplined army to meet the German advance, but it had something infinitely more effective: it had a conscious revolutionary people who would have fought back the invaders to the last drop of blood. As a matter of fact, it was the people who had checked all the counter-revolutionary military attempts against Russia. Who else but the people, the peasants and the workers, made it impossible for the German and Austrian army to remain in the Ukraine? Who defeated Denikin and the other counter-revolutionary generals? Who triumphed over Koltchak and Yudenitch? Lenin and Trotsky claim that it was the Red Army. But the historic truth was that the voluntary military units of the workers and peasants—the *povstantsi*—in Siberia as well as in the south of Russia—had borne the brunt of the fighting on every front, the Red Army usually only completing the victories of the former. Trotsky would have it now that the Brest treaty had to be accepted, but he himself had at one time refused to sign the treaty and Radek, Joffe, and other leading Communists had also been opposed to it. It is claimed now that they submitted to the shameful terms because they realized the hopelessness of their expectation that the German workers would prevent the Junkers from marching against revolutionary Russia. But that was not the true reason. It was the whip of the party discipline which lashed Trotsky and others into submission.

"The trouble with the Bolsheviki," continued Spiridonova, "is that they have no faith in the masses. They proclaimed themselves a proletarian party, but they refused to trust the workers." It was this lack of faith, Maria emphasized, which made the Communists bow to German imperialism. And as concerns the Revolution itself, it was precisely the Brest peace which struck it a fatal blow. Aside from

mercy of the German Junkers by the Brest peace—the peasants saw thousands of their brothers slain, and had to submit to being robbed and plundered. The simple peasant mind could not understand the complete reversal of the former Bolshevik slogans of "no indemnity and no annexations." But even the simplest peasant could understand that his toil and his blood were to pay the indemnities imposed by the Brest conditions. The peasants grew bitter and antagonistic to the Soviet régime. Disheartened and discouraged they turned from the Revolution. As to the effect of the Brest peace upon the German workers, how could they continue in their faith in the Russian Revolution in view of the fact that the Bolsheviki negotiated and accepted the peace terms with the German masters over the heads of the German proletariat? The historic fact remains that the Brest peace was the beginning of the end of the Russian Revolution. No doubt other factors contributed to the debacle, but Brest was the most fatal of them.

Spiridonova asserted that the Left Socialist Revolutionary elements had warned the Bol sheviki against that peace and fought it desperately. They refused to accept it even after it had been signed. The presence of Mirbach in Revolutionary Russia they considered an outrage against the Revolution, a crying injustice to the heroic Russian people who had sacrificed and suffered so much in their struggle against imperialism and capitalism. Spiridonova's party decided that Mirbach could not be tolerated in Russia: Mirbach had to go. Wholesale arrests and persecutions followed upon the execution of Mirbach, the Bolsheviki rendering service to the German Kaiser. They filled the prisons with the Russian revolutionists.

In the course of our conversation I suggested that the method of *razverstka* was probably forced upon the Bolsheviki by the refusal of the peasants to feed the city. In the beginning of the revolutionary period, Spiridonova explained, so long as the peasant Soviets existed, the peasants gave willingly and generously. But when the Bolshevik Government began to dissolve these Soviets and arrested 500 peasant delegates, the peasantry became antagonistic. Moreover, they daily witnessed the inefficiency of the Communist régime: they saw their products lying at side stations and rotting away,

continue to give. The fact that the peasants had never refused to contribute supplies to the Red Army proved that other methods than those used by the Bolsheviki could have been employed. The *razverstka* served only to widen the breach between the village and the city. The Bolsheviki resorted to punitive expeditions which became the terror of the country. They left death and ruin wherever they came. The peasants, at last driven to desperation, began to rebel against the Communist régime. In various parts of Russia, in the south, on the Ural, and in Siberia, peasants' insurrections have taken place, and everywhere they were being put down by force of arms and with an iron hand.

Spiridonova did not speak of her own sufferings since she had parted ways with the Bolsheviki. But I learned from others that she had been arrested twice and imprisoned for a considerable length of time. Even when free she was kept under surveillance, as she had been in the time of the Tsar. On several occasions she was tortured by being taken out at night and informed that she was to be shot—a favoured Tcheka method. I mentioned the subject to

Spiridonova. She did not deny the facts, though she was loath to speak of herself. She was entirely absorbed in the fate of the Revolution and of her beloved peasantry. She gave no thought to herself, but she was eager to have the world and the international proletariat learn the true condition of affairs in Bolshevik Russia.

Of all the opponents of the Bolsheviki I had met Maria Spiridonova impressed me as one of the most sincere, well-poised, and convincing. Her heroic past and her refusal to compromise her revolutionary ideas under Tsarism as well as under Bolshevism were sufficient guarantee of her revolutionary integrity.

CHAPTER XVII

ANOTHER VISIT TO PETER KROPOTKIN

A FEW days before our Expedition started for the Ukraine the opportunity presented itself to pay another visit to Peter Kropotkin. I was delighted at the chance to see the dear old man under more favourable conditions than I had seen him in March. I expected at least that we would not be handicapped by the presence of newspaper men as we were on the previous occasion.

On my first visit, in snow-clad March, I arrived at the Kropotkin cottage late in the evening. The place looked deserted and desolate. But now it was summer time. The country was fresh and fragrant; the garden at the back of the house, clad in green, smiled cheerfully, the golden rays of the sun spreading warmth and light. Peter, who was having his afternoon nap, could not be seen, but Sofya Grigorievna, his wife, was there to greet us. We had brought some provisions given to Sasha

Kropotkin for her father, and several baskets of things sent by an Anarchist group. While we were unpacking those treasures Peter Alekseyevitch surprised us. He seemed a changed man: the summer had wrought a miracle in him. He appeared healthier, stronger, more alive than when I had last seen him. He immediately took us to the vegetable garden which was almost entirely Sofya's own work and served as the main support of the family. Peter was very proud of it. "What do you say to this!" he exclaimed; "all Sofya's labour. And see this new species of lettuce"—pointing at a huge head. He looked young; he was almost gay, his conversation sparkling. His power of observation, his keen sense of humour and generous humanity were so refreshing, he made one forget the misery of Russia, one's own conflicts and doubts, and the cruel reality of life.

After dinner we gathered in Peter's study— a small room containing an ordinary table for a desk, a narrow cot, a wash-stand, and shelves of books. I could not help making a mental comparison between this simple, cramped study of Kropotkin and the gorgeous quarters of Radek and Zinoviev. Peter was interested to know my impressions since he saw me last. I related to him how confused and harassed I was, how everything seemed to crumble beneath my feet. I told him that I had come to doubt almost everything, even the Revolution itself. I could not reconcile the ghastly reality with what the Revolution had meant to me when I came to Russia. Were the conditions I found inevitable—the callous indifference to human life, the terrorism, the waste and agony of it all? Of course, I knew revolutions could not be made with kid gloves. It is a stern necessity involving violence and destruction, a difficult and terrible process. But what I had found in Russia was utterly unlike revolutionary conditions, so fundamentally unlike as to be a caricature.

Peter listened attentively; then he said: "There is no reason whatever to lose faith. I consider the Russian Revolution even greater than the French, for it has struck deeper into the soul of Russia, into the hearts and minds of the Russian people. Time alone can demonstrate its full scope and depth. What you see to-day is only the surface, conditions artificially created by a governing class. You see a small political party which by its false theories, blunders, and inefficiency has demonstrated how revolutions

must *not* be made." It was unfortunate—
Kropotkin continued—that so many of the
Anarchists in Russia and the masses outside of
Russia had been carried away by the ultra-
revolutionary pretenses of the Bolsheviki. In
the great upheaval it was forgotten that the
Communists are a political party firmly adher
ing to the idea of a centralized State, and that as
such they were bound to misdirect the course of
the Revolution. The Bolsheviki were the Je
suits of the Socialist Church: they believed in
the Jesuitic motto that the end justifies the
means. Their end being political power, they
hesitate at nothing. The means, however, have
paralysed the energies of the masses and have
terrorized the people. Yet without the people,
without the direct participation of the masses
in the reconstruction of the country, nothing
essential could be accomplished. The Bolsheviki had been carried to the top by the high
tide of the Revolution. Once in power they
began to stem the tide   They have been trying
to eliminate and suppress the cultural forces of
the country not entirely in agreement with their
ideas and methods. They destroyed the co-
operatives which were of utmost importance to
the life of Russia, the great link between the

country and the city. They created a bureaucracy and officialdom which surpasses even that
of the old régime. In the village where he lived,
in little Dmitrov, there were more Bolshevik
officials than ever existed there during the reign
of the Romanovs. All those people were living
off the masses. They were parasites on the
social body, and Dmitrov was only a small ex-
ample of what was going on throughout Russia.
It was not the fault of any particular individuals:
rather was it the State they had created, which
discredits every revolutionary ideal, stifles all
initiative, and sets a premium on incompetence
and waste. It should also not be forgotten,
Kropotkin emphasized, that the blockade and
the continuous attacks on the Revolution by the
interventionists had helped to strengthen the
power of the Communist régime. Interven
tion and blockade were bleeding Russia to death,
and were preventing the people from understanding the real nature of the Bolshevik
régime.

Discussing the activities and rôle of the
Anarchists in the Revolution, Kropotkin said:
"We Anarchists have talked much of revolutions, but few of us have been prepared for the
actual work to be done during the process. I

have indicated some things in this relation in my 'Conquest of Bread.' Pouget and Pataud have also sketched a line of action in their work on 'How to Accomplish the Social Revolution.'" Kropotkin thought that the Anarchists had not given sufficient consideration to the fundamental elements of the social revolution. The real facts in a revolutionary process do not consist so much in the actual fighting—that is, merely the destructive phase necessary to clear the way for constructive effort. The basic factor in a revolution is the organization of the economic life of the country. The Russian Revolution had proved conclusively that we must prepare thoroughly for that. Everything else is of minor importance. He had come to think that syndicalism was likely to furnish what Russia most lacked: the channel through which the industrial and economic reconstruction of the country may flow. He referred to Anarcho-syndicalism. That and the co-operatives would save other countries· some of the blunders and suffering Russia was going through.

I left Dmitrov much comforted by the warmth and light which the beautiful personality of Peter Kropotkin radiated; and I was much

CHAPTER XVIII

EN ROUTE

OUR train was about to leave Moscow when we were surprised by an interesting visitor—Krasnoschekov, the president of the Far Eastern Republic, who had recently arrived in the capital from Siberia. He had heard of our presence in the city, but for some reason he could not locate us. Finally he met Alexander Berkman who invited him to the Museum car.

In appearance Krasnoschekov had changed tremendously since his Chicago days, when, known as Tobinson, he was superintendent of the Workers' Institute in that city. Then he was one of the many Russian emigrants on the West Side, active as organizer and lecturer in the Socialist movement. Now he looked a different man; his expression stern, the stamp of authority on him, he seemed even to have grown taller. But at heart he remained the same—simple and kind, the Tobinson we had known in Chicago.

the conditions in the Far East and the local form of government. It consisted of representatives of various political factions and "even Anarchists are with us," said Krasnoschekov; "thus, for instance, Shatov is Minister of Railways. We are independent in the East and there is free speech. Come over and try us, you will find a field for your work." He invited Alexander Berkman and myself to visit him in Chita and we assured him that we hoped to avail ourselves of the invitation at some future time. He seemed to have brought a different atmosphere and we were sorry to part so soon.

On the way from Petrograd to Moscow the Expedition had been busy putting its house in order. As already mentioned, the car consisted of six compartments, two of which were converted into a dining room and kitchen. They were of diminutive size, but we managed to make a presentable dining room of one, and the kitchen might have made many a housekeeper envy us. A large Russian samovar and all necessary copper and zinc pots and kettles were there, making a very effective appearance. We were especially proud of the decorative curtains on our car windows. The other compartments were used for office and sleeping quarters. I shared mine with our secretary, Miss A. T. Shakol.

Besides Alexander Berkman, appointed by the Museum as chairman and general manager, Shakol as secretary, and myself as treasurer and housekeeper, the Expedition consisted of three other members, including a young Communist, a student of the Petrograd University. En route we mapped out our plan of work, each member of the Expedition being assigned some particular branch of it. I was to gather data in the Departments of Education and Health, the Bureaus of Social Welfare and Labour Distribution, as well as in the organization known as Workers' and Peasants' Inspection. After the day's work all the members were to meet in the car to consider and classify the material collected during the day.

Our first stop was Kursk. Nothing of importance was collected there except a pair of *kandai* [iron handcuffs] which had been worn by a revolutionist in Schlüsselburg. It was donated to us by a chance passer-by who, noticing the inscription on our car, "Extraordinary Commission of the Museum of the Revolution," became interested and called to pay us a visit. He proved to be an intellectual, a Tolstoian, the manager of a children's colony. He succeeded in maintaining the latter by giving the Soviet Government a certain amount of labour required of him: three days a week he taught in the Soviet schools of Kursk. The rest of his time he devoted to his little colony, or the "Children's Commune," as he affectionately called it. With the help of the children and some adults they raised the vegetables necessary for the support of the colony and made all the repairs of the place. He stated that he had not been directly interfered with by the Government, but that his work was considerably handicapped by discrimination against him as a pacifist and Tolstoian. He feared that because of it his place could not be continued much longer. There was no trading of any sort in Kursk at the time, and one had to depend for supplies on the local authorities. But discrimination and antagonism manifested themselves against independent initiative and effort. The Tolstoian, however, was determined to make a fight, spiritually speaking, for the life of his colony. He was planning to go to the centre, to Moscow, where he hoped to get support in favour of his commune.

The personality of the man, his eagerness to make himself useful, did not correspond with the information I had received from Communists about the *intelligentsia*, their indifference and unwillingness to help revolutionary Russia. I broached the subject to our visitor. He could only speak of the professional men and women of Kursk, his native city, but he assured us that he found most of them, and especially the teachers, eager to coöperate and even self-sacrificing. But they were the most neglected class, living in semi-starvation all the time. Like himself, they were exposed to general antagonism, even on the part of the children whose minds had been poisoned by agitation against the *intelligentsia*.

Kursk is a large industrial centre and I was interested in the fate of the workers there. We learned from our visitor that there had been repeated skirmishes between the workers and the Soviet authorities. A short time before our arrival a strike had broken out and soldiers were sent to quell it. The usual arrests followed and many workers were still in the Tcheka. This state of affairs, the Tolstoian thought, was due to general Communist incompetence rather than to any other cause. People were placed in responsible positions not because of their fitness but owing to their party membership. Political usefulness was the first consideration and it naturally resulted in general abuse of power and confusion. The Communist dogma that the end justifies all means was also doing much harm. It had thrown the door wide open to the worst human passions, and discredited the ideals of the Revolution. The Tolstoian spoke sadly, as one speaks of a hope cherished and loved, and lost.

The next morning our visitor donated to our collection the *kandali* he had worn for many years in prison. He hoped that we might return by way of Kursk so that we could pay a visit to some Tolstoian communes in the environs of the city. Not far from Yasnaya Polyana there lived an old peasant friend of Tolstoi, he told us. He had much valuable material that he might contribute to the Museum. Our visitor remained to the moment of our departure; he was starved for intellectual companionship and was loath to see us go.

CHAPTER XIX

IN KHARKOV

ARRIVING in Kharkov, I visited the Anarchist book store, the address of which I had secured in Moscow. There I met many friends whom I had known in America. Among them were Joseph and Leah Goodman, formerly from Detroit; Fanny Baron, from Chicago, and Sam Fleshin who had worked in the Mother Earth office in New York, in 1917, before he left for Russia. With thousands of other exiles they had all hastened to their native country at the first news of the Revolution, and they had been in the thick of it ever since. They would have much to tell me, I thought; they might help me to solve some of the problems that were perplexing me.

Kharkov lay several miles away from the railroad station, and it would have therefore been impractical to continue living in the car during our stay in the city. The Museum credentials would secure quarters for us, but several mem bers of the Expedition preferred to stay with their American friends. Through the help of one of our comrades, who was commandant of an apartment house, I secured a room.

It had been quite warm in Moscow, but Kharkov proved a veritable furnace, reminding me of New York in July. Sanitary and plumbing arrangements had been neglected or destroyed, and water had to be carried from a place several blocks distant up three flights of stairs. Still it was a comfort to have a private room.

The city was alive. The streets were full of people and they looked better fed and dressed than the population of Petrograd and Moscow. The women were handsomer than in northern Russia; the men of a finer type. It was rather odd to see beautiful women, wearing evening gowns in the daytime, walk about barefoot or clad in wooden sandals without stockings. The coloured kerchiefs most of them had on lent life and colour to the streets, giving them a cheerful appearance which contrasted favourably with the gray tones of Petrograd.

My first official visit was paid to the Department of Education. I found a long line of people waiting admission, but the Museum credentials immediately opened the doors, the chairman receiving me most cordially. He listened attentively to my explanation of the purposes of the Expedition and promised to give me an opportunity to collect all the available material in his department, including the newly prepared charts of its work. On the chairman's desk I noticed a copy of such a chart, looking like a futurist picture, all lined and dotted with red, blue, and purple. Noticing my puzzled expression the chairman explained that the red indicated the various phases of the educational system, the other colours representing literature, drama, music, and the plastic arts. Each department was subdivided into bureaus embracing every branch of the educational and cultural work of the Socialist Republic.

Concerning the system of education the chairman stated that from three to eight years of age the child attended the kindergarten or children's home. War orphans from the south, children of Red Army soldiers and of proletarians in general received preference. If vacancies remained, children of the bourgeoisie were also accepted. From eight to thirteen the children attended the intermediary schools where they received elementary education which inculcates the general idea of the political and economic structure of R.S.F.

S.R. Modern methods of instruction by means of technical apparatus, so far as the latter could be secured, had been introduced. The children were taught processes of production as well as natural sciences. The period from twelve to seventeen embraced vocational training. There were also higher institutions of learning for young people who showed special ability and inclination. Besides this, summer schools and colonies had been established where instruction was given in the open. All children belonging to the Soviet Republic were fed, clothed, and housed at the expense of the Government. The scheme of education also embraced workers' colleges and evening courses for adults of both sexes. Here also everything was supplied to the pupils free, even special rations. For further particulars the chairman referred me to the literature of his department and advised me to study the plan in operation. The educational work was much handicapped by the blockade and counter-revolutionary attempts; else Russia would demonstrate to the world what the Socialist Republic could do in the way of popular enlightenment. They lacked even the most elemental necessaries, such as paper, pencils, and books. In the winter most of the schools had to be closed for lack of fuel. The cruelty and infamy of the blockade was nowhere more apparent and crying than in its effect upon the sick and the children. "It is the blackest crime of the century," the chairman concluded. It was agreed that I return within a week to receive the material for our collection. In the Social Welfare Department I also found a very competent man in charge. He became much interested in the work of the Expedition and promised to collect the necessary material for us, though he could not offer very much because his department had but recently been organized. Its work was to look after the disabled and sick proletarians and those of old age exempt from labour. They were given certain rations in food and clothing; in case they were employed they received also a certain amount of money, about half of their earnings. Besides that the Department was supporting living quarters and dining rooms for its charges.

In the corridor leading to the various offices of the Department there were lines of emaciated and crippled figures, men and women, waiting for their turn to receive aid. They looked like war veterans awaiting their pittance in the form of rations; they reminded me of the decrepit unemployed standing in line in the Salvation

Army quarters in America. One woman in particular attracted my attention. She was angry and excited and she complained loudly. Her husband had been dead two days and she was trying to obtain a permit for a coffin. She had been in line ever since but could procure no order. "What am I to do?" she wailed; "I cannot carry him on my own back or bury him without a coffin, and I cannot keep him in my room much longer in this heat." The woman's lament remained unanswered for everyone was absorbed in his own troubles. Sick and disabled workers are thrown everywhere on the scrap pile—I thought—but in Russia an effort is being made to prevent such cruelty. Yet judging from what I saw in Kharkov I felt that not much was being accomplished. It was a most depressing picture, that long waiting line. I felt as if it was adding insult to injury.

I visited a house where the social derelicts lived. It was fairly well kept, but breathing the spirit of cold institutionalism. It was, of course, better than sleeping in the streets or lying all night in the doorways, as the sick and poor are often compelled to do in capitalist countries, in America, for instance. Still it seemed incongruous that something more cheerful and inviting

could not be devised in Soviet Russia for those
who had sacrificed their health and had given
their labour to the common good. But apparently it was the best that the Social Welfare
Department could do in the present condition
of Russia.

In the evening our American friends visited
us. Each of them had a rich experience of struggle, suffering, and persecution and I was surprised to learn that most of them had also been
imprisoned by the Bolsheviki. They had endured much for the sake of their ideas and had
been hounded by every government of Ukraina,
there having been fourteen political changes in
some parts of the south during the last two years.
The Communists were no different: they also
persecuted the Anarchists as well as other revolutionists of the Left. Still the Anarchists
continued their work. Their faith in the Revolution, in spite of all they endured, and even in
the face of the worst reaction, was truly sublime.
They agreed that the possibilities of the masses
during the first months after the October Revolution were very great, but expressed the opinion that revolutionary development had been
checked, and gradually entirely paralysed, by
the deadening effect of the Communist State.

In the Ukraina, they explained, the situation differed from that of Russia, because the peasants lived in comparatively better material conditions. They had also retained greater independence and more of a rebellious spirit. For these reasons the Bolsheviki had failed to subdue the south.

Our visitors spoke of Makhno as a heroic popular figure, and related his daring exploits and the legends the peasants had woven about his personality. There was considerable difference of opinion, however, among the Anarchists concerning the significance of the Makhno movement. Some regarded it as expressive of Anarchism and believed that the Anarchists should devote all their energies to it. Others held that the *povstantsi* represented the native rebellious spirit of the southern peasants, but that their movement was not Anarchism, though anarchistically tinged. They were not in favour of limiting themselves to that movement; they believed their work should be of a more embracing and universal character. Several of our friends took an entirely different position, denying to the Makhno movement any anarchistic meaning whatever.

Most enthusiastic about Makhno and emphatic about the Anarchist value of that movement was Joseph, known as the "Emigrant"— the very last man one would have expected to wax warm over a military organization. Joseph was as mild and gentle as a girl. In America he had participated in the Anarchist and Labour movements in a quiet and unassuming manner, and very few knew the true worth of the man. Since his return to Russia he had been in the thick of the struggle. He had spent much time with Makhno and had learned to love and admire him for his revolutionary devotion and courage. Joseph related an interesting experience of his first visit to the peasant leader. When he arrived the *povstantsi* for some reason conceived the notion that he had come to harm their chief. One of Makhno's closest friends claimed that Joseph, being a Jew, must also be an emissary of the Bolsheviki sent to kill Makhno. When he saw how attached Makhno became to Joseph, he decided to kill "the Jew." Fortunately he first warned his leader, whereupon Makhno called his men together and addressed them somewhat in this manner: "Joseph is a Jew and an idealist; he is an Anarchist. I consider him my comrade and friend and I shall hold everyone responsible for his safety." Idolized

Joseph became the trusted friend of the *povstantsi*. They believed in him because their *batka* [father] had faith in him, and Joseph in return became deeply devoted to them. Now he insisted that he must return to the rebel camp· they were heroic people, simple, brave, and devoted to the cause of liberty. He was planning to join Makhno again. Yet I could not free myself of the feeling that if Joseph went back I should never see him alive any more. He seemed to me like one of those characters in Zola's "Germinal" who loves every living thing and yet is able to resort to dynamite for the sake of the striking miners.

I expressed the view to my friends that, important as the Makhno movement might be, it was of a purely military nature and could not, therefore, be expressive of the Anarchist spirit. I was sorry to see Joseph return to the Makhno. camp, for his work for the Anarchist movement in Russia could be of much greater value. But he was determined, and I felt that it was Joseph's despair at the reactionary tendencies of the Bolsheviki which drove him, as it did so many others of his comrades, away from the Communists and into the ranks of Makhno.

During our stay in Kharkov I also visited the Department of Labour Distribution, which had come into existence since the militarization of labour. According to the Bolsheviki it became necessary then to return the workers from the villages to which they had streamed from the starving cities. They had to be registered and classified according to trades and distributed to points where their services were most needed. In the carrying out of this plan many people were daily rounded up on the streets and in the market place. Together with the large numbers arrested as speculators or for possession of Tsarist money, they were put on the list of the Labour Distribution Department. Some were sent to the Donetz Basin, while the weaker ones went on to concentration camps. The Communists justified this system and method as necessary during a revolutionary period in order to build up the industries. Everybody must work in Russia, they said, or be forced to work. They claimed that the industrial output had increased since the introduction of the compulsory labour law.

I had occasion to discuss these matters with many Communists and I doubted the efficacy of the new policy.

tionalized she was allowed to keep three rooms, the rest of her apartment having been put in charge of the House Bureau. Her family consisted of eight members, including her parents and a married daughter with her family. It was almost impossible to crowd all into three rooms, especially considering the terrific heat of the Kharkov summer; yet somehow they had managed. But two weeks prior to our arrival in Kharkov Zinoviev visited the city. At a public meeting he declared that the bourgeoisie of the city looked too well fed and dressed. "It proves," he said, "that the comrades and especially the Tcheka are neglecting their duty." No sooner had Zinoviev departed than wholesale arrests and night raids began. Confiscation became the order of the day. Her apartment, the woman related, had also been visited and most of her effects taken away. But worst of all was that the Tcheka ordered her to vacate one of the rooms, and now the whole family was crowded into two small rooms. She was much worried lest a member of the Tcheka or a Red Army man be assigned to the vacant room.

"We felt much relieved," she said, "when we were informed that someone from America was to occupy this room. We wish you would remain here for a long time."

Till then I had not come in personal contact with the members of the expropriated bourgeoisie who had actually been made to suffer by the Revolution. The few middle-class families I had met lived well, which was a source of surprise to me. Thus in Petrograd a certain chemist I had become acquainted with in Shatov's house lived in a very expensive way. The Soviet authorities permitted him to operate his factory, and he supplied the Government with chemicals at a cost much less than the Government could manufacture them at. He paid his workers comparatively high wages and provided them with rations. On a certain occasion I was invited to dinner by the chemist's family. I found them living in a luxurious apartment containing many valuable objects and art treasures. My hostess, the chemist's wife, was expensively gowned and wore a costly necklace. Dinner consisted of several courses and was served in an extravagant manner with exquisite damask linen in abundance. It must have cost several hundred thousand rubles, everybody in Petrograd knew the chemist and was familiar with his mode of life. But I was informed that he was needed by the Soviet Government and that he was therefore permitted to live as he pleased. Once I expressed my surprise to him that the Bolsheviki had not confiscated his wealth. He assured me that he was not the only one of the bourgeoisie who had retained his former condition. "The bourgeoisie is by no means dead," he said; "it has only been chloroformed for a while, so to speak, for the painful operation. But it is already recovering from the effect of the anesthetic and soon it will have recuperated entirely. It only needs a little more time." The woman who visited me in the Kharkov room had not managed so well as the Petrograd chemist. She was a part of the wreckage left by the revolutionary storm that had swept over Russia.

During my stay in the Ukrainian capital I met some interesting people of the professional classes, among them an engineer who had just returned from the Donetz Basin and a woman employed in a Soviet Bureau. Both were cultured persons and keenly alive to the fate of Russia. We discussed the Zinoviev visit. They corroborated the story told me before. Zinoviev had upbraided his comrades for their laxity toward the bourgeoisie and criticized them for not suppressing trade. Immediately upon Zinoviev's departure the Tcheka began indiscriminate raids, the members of the bourgeoisie losing on that occasion almost the last things they possessed. The most tragic part of it, according to the engineer, was that the workers did not benefit by such raids. No one knew what became of the things confiscated—they just disappeared. Both the engineer and the woman Soviet employee spoke with much concern about the general disintegration of ideas. The Russians once believed, the woman said, that hovels and palaces were equally wrong and should be abolished. It never occurred to them that the purpose of a revolution is merely to cause a transfer of possessions—to put the rich into the hovels and the poor into the palaces. It was not true that the workers have gotten into the palaces. They were only made to believe that that is the function of a revolution. In reality, the masses remained where they had been before. But now they were not alone there: they were in the company of the classes they meant to destroy.

The civil engineer had been sent by the Soviet Government to the Donetz Basin to build homes for the workers, and I was glad of the opportunity to learn from him about the conditions there. The Communist press was publishing glowing accounts about the intensive coal production of the Basin, and official calculations claimed that the country would be provided with sufficient coal for the approaching winter. In reality, the Donetz mines were in a most deplorable state, the engineer informed me. The miners were herded like cattle. They received abominable rations, were almost barefoot, and were forced to work standing in water up to their ankles. As a result of such conditions very little coal was being produced. "I was one of a committee ordered to investigate the situation and report our findings," said the engineer. "Our report is far from favourable. We know that it is dangerous to relate the facts as we found them: it may land us in the Tcheka. But we decided that Moscow must face the facts. The system of political Commissars, general Bolshevik inefficiency, and the paralysing effect of the State machinery have made our constructive work in the Basin almost impossible. It was a dismal failure."

Could such a condition of affairs be avoided in a revolutionary period and in a country so little developed industrially as Russia? I questioned. The Revolution was being attacked by the bourgeoisie within and without; there was compelling need of defence and no energies remained for constructive work The engineer scorned my viewpoint. The Russian bourgeoisie was weak and could offer practically no resistance, he claimed. It was numerically insignificant and it suffered from a sick conscience. There was neither need nor justification for Bolshevik terrorism and it was mainly the latter that paralysed the constructive efforts. Middle-class intellectuals had been active for many years in the liberal and revolutionary movements of Russia, and thus the members of the bourgeoisie had become closer to the masses. When the great day arrived the bourgeoisie, caught unawares, preferred to give up rather than to put up a fight. It was stunned by the Revolution more than any other class in Russia. It was quite unprepared and has not gotten its bearings even to this day. It was not true, as the Bolsheviki claimed, that the Russian bourgeoisie was an active menace to the Revolution.

I had been advised to see the Chief of the Department of Workers' and Peasants' Inspection, the position being held by a woman, formerly an officer of the Tcheka, reputed to be very severe, even cruel, but efficient. She could supply me with much valuable material, I was told, and give me entrance to the prisons and concentration camps. On my visiting the Workers' and Peasants' Inspection offices I found the lady in charge not at all cordial at first. She ignored my credentials, apparently not impressed by Zinoviev's signature. Presently a man stepped out from an inner office. He proved to be Dibenko, a high Red Army officer, and he informed me that he had heard of me from Alexandra Kollontay, whom he referred to as his wife. He promised that I should get all available material and asked me to return later in the day When I called again I found the lady much more amiable and willing to give me information about the activities of her department. It appeared that the latter had been organized to fight growing sabotage and graft. It was part of the duties of the Tcheka, but it was found necessary to create the new department for the inspection and correction of abuses. "It is the tribunal to which cases may be appealed," said the woman; "just now, for instance, we are investigating complaints of prisoners who had been wrongly convicted or received excessive sentences." She promised to secure for us permission to inspect the penal institutions and several days later several members of the Expedition were given the opportunity.

First we visited the main concentration camp of Kharkov. We found a number of prisoners working in the yard, digging a new sewer. It was certainly needed, for the whole place was filled with nauseating smells. The prison build ing was divided into a number of rooms, all of them overcrowded. One of the compartments was called the "speculators' apartment," though almost all its inmates protested against being thus classed. They looked poor and starved, everyone of them anxious to tell us his tale of woe, apparently under the impression that we were official investigators. In one of the corridors we found several Communists charged with sabotage. Evidently the Soviet Government did not discriminate in favour of its own people.

There were in the camp White officers taken prisoners at the Polish front, and scores of peasant men and women held on various charges. They presented a pitiful sight, sitting there on the floor for lack of benches, a pathetic lot, bewildered and unable to grasp the combination of events which had caught them in the net.

More than one thousand able-bodied men were locked up in the concentration camp, of no serv ice to the community and requiring numerous officials to guard and attend them. And yet Russia was badly in need of labour energy. It seemed to me an impractical waste.

Later we visited the prison. At the gates an angry mob was gesticulating and shouting. I learned that the weekly parcels brought by relatives of the inmates had that morning been refused acceptance by the prison authorities. Some of the people had come for miles and had spent their last ruble for food for their arrested husbands and brothers. They were frantic. Our escort, the woman in charge of the Bureau, promised to investigate the matter. We made the rounds of the big prison—a depressing sight of human misery and despair. In the solitary were those condemned to death. For days their look haunted me—their eyes full of terror at the torturing uncertainty, fearing to be called at any moment to face death.

We had been asked by our Kharkov friends to find a certain young woman in the prison. Trying to avoid arousing attention we sought her with our eyes in various parts of the institution, till we saw someone answering her description. She was an Anarchist, held as a political. The prison conditions were bad, she told us. It had required a protracted hunger strike to compel the authorities to treat the politicals more decently and to keep the doors of those condemned to death open during the day, so that they could receive a little cheer and comfort from the other prisoners. She told of many unjustly arrested and pointed out an old stupid-looking peasant-woman locked up in solitary as a Makhno spy, a charge obviously due to a misunderstanding.

The prison régime was very rigid. Among other things, it was forbidden the prisoners to climb up on the windows or to look out into the yard. The story was related to us of a prisoner being shot for once disobeying that rule. He had heard some noise in the street below and, curious to know what was going on, he climbed up on the window sill of his cell. The sentry in the yard gave no warning. He fired, severely wounding the man. Many similar stories of severity and abuse we heard from the prisoners. On our way to town I expressed surprise at the conditions that were being tolerated in the prisons. I remarked to our guide that it would cause a serious scandal if the western world were to learn under what conditions prisoners live and how they are treated in Socialist Russia. Nothing could justify such brutality, I thought. But the chairman of the Workers' and Peasants' Inspection remained unmoved. "We are living in a revolutionary period," she replied; "these matters cannot be helped." But she promised to investigate some cases of extreme injustice which we had pointed out to her. I was not convinced that the Revolution was responsible for the existing evils. If the Revolution really had to support so much brutality and crime, what was the purpose of the Revolution, after all?

At the end of our first week in Kharkov I returned to the Department of Education where I had been promised material. To my surprise I found that nothing had been prepared. I was informed that the chairman was absent, and again assured that the promised data would be collected and ready before our departure. I was then referred to the man in charge of a certain school experimental department. The chairman had told me that some interesting educational methods were being developed, but I found the manager unintelligent and dull. He could tell me nothing of the new methods, but he was willing to send for one of the instructors to explain things to me. A messenger was dispatched, but he soon returned with the information that the teacher was busy demonstrating to his class and could not come. The manager flew into a rage. "He must come," he shouted; "the bourgeoisie are sabotaging like the other damnable *intelligentsia*. They ought all to be shot. We can do very well without them." He was one of the type of narrow-minded fanatical and persecuting Communists who did more harm to the Revolution than any counter-revolutionary.

During our stay in Kharkov we also had time to visit some factories. In a plough manufacturing plant we found a large loft stacked with the finished product. I was surprised that the ploughs were kept in the factory instead of being put to practical use on the farms. "We are awaiting orders from Moscow,' the manager explained; "it was a rush order and we were threatened with arrest for sabotage in case it should not be ready for shipment within six weeks. That was six months ago, and as you see the ploughs are still here. ' The peasants need them badly, and we need their bread. But we cannot exchange. We must await orders from Moscow."

I recalled a remark of Zinoviev when on our first meeting he stated that Petrograd lacked fuel, notwithstanding the fact that less than a hundred versts from the city there was enough to supply almost half the country. I suggested on that occasion that the workers of Petrograd be called upon to get the fuel to the city. Zinoviev thought it very naïve. "Should we grant such a thing in Petrograd," he said, "the same demand would be made in other cities. It would create communal competition which is a bourgeois institution. It would interfere with our plan of nationalized and centralized control" That was the dominating principle, and as a result of it the Kharkov workers lacked bread until Moscow should give orders to have the ploughs sent to the peasants. The supremacy of the State was the cornerstone of Marxism.

Several days before leaving Kharkov I once more visited the Board of Education and again I failed to find its chairman. To my consternation I was informed that I would receive no material because it had been decided that

Ukraina was to have its own museum and the chairman had gone to Kiev to organize it. I felt indignant at the miserable deception practised upon us by a man in high Communist position. Surely Ukraina had the right to have its own museum, but why this petty fraud which caused the Expedition to lose so much valuable time.

The sequel to this incident came a few days later when we were surprised by the hasty arrival of our secretary who informed us that we must leave Kharkov immediately and as quietly as possible, because the local executive committee of the party had decided to prevent our carrying out statistical material from Ukraina. Accordingly, we made haste to leave in order to save what we had already collected. We knew the material would be lost if it remained in Kharkov and that the plan of an independent Ukrainian museum would for many years remain only on paper.

Before departing we made arrangements for a last conference with our local friends. We felt that we might never see them again. On that occasion the work of the "Nabat" Federation was discussed in detail. That general Anarchist organization of the south had been founded as a result of the experiences of the Russian Anarchists and the conviction that a unified body was necessary to make their work more effective. They wanted not merely to die but to live for the Revolution. It appeared that the Anarchists of Russia had been divided into several factions, most of them numerically small and of little practical influence upon the progress of events in Russia. They had been unable to establish a permanent hold in the ranks of the workers. It was therefore decided to gather all the Anarchist elements of the Ukraina into one federation and thus be in condition to present a solid front in the struggle not only against invasion and counter-revolution, but also against Communist persecution.

By means of unified effort the "Nabat" was able to cover most of the south and get in close touch with the life of the workers and the peasantry. The frequent changes of government in the Ukraina finally drove the Anarchists to cover, the relentless persecution of the Bolsheviki having depleted their ranks of the most active workers. Still the Federation had taken root among the people. The little band was in constant danger, but it was energetically continuing its educational and propaganda work.

The Kharkov Anarchists had evidently expected much from our presence in Russia. They hoped that Alexander Berkman and myself would join them in their work. We were already seven months in Russia but had as yet taken no direct part in the Anarchist movement. I could sense the disappointment and impatience of our comrades. They were eager we should at least inform the European and American Anarchists of what was going on in Russia, particularly about the ruthless persecution of the Left revolutionary elements. Well could I understand the attitude of my Ukrainian friends. They had suffered much during the last years: they had seen the high hopes of the Revolution crushed and Russia breaking down beneath the heel of the Bolshevik State. Yet I could not comply with their wishes. I still had faith in the Bolsheviki, in their revolutionary sincerity and integrity. Moreover, I felt that as long as Russia was being attacked from the outside I could not speak in criticism. I would not add fuel to the fires of counter-revolution. I therefore had to keep silent, and stand by the Bolsheviki as the organized defenders of the Revolution. But my Russian friends scorned this view. I was confounding

said; they were not the same; on the contrary, they were opposed, even antagonistic. The Communist State, according to the "Nabat" Anarchists, had proven fatal to the Revolution.

Within a few hours before our departure we received the confidential information that Makhno had sent a call for Alexander Berkman and myself to visit him. He wished to place his situation before us, and, through us, before the Anarchist movement of the world. He desired to have it widely understood that he was not the bandit, Jew-baiter, and counter-revolutionist the Bolsheviki had proclaimed him. He was devoted to the Revolution and was serving the interests of the people as he conceived them.

It was a great temptation to meet the modern Stenka Rasin, but we were pledged to the Museum and could not break faith with the other members of the Expedition.

CHAPTER XX

POLTAVA

IN THE general dislocation of life in Russia and the breaking down of her economic machinery the railroad system had suffered most. The subject was discussed in almost every meeting and every Soviet paper often wrote about it. Between Petrograd and Moscow, however, the real state of affairs was not so noticeable, though the main stations were always overcrowded and the people waited for days trying to secure places. Still, trains between Petrograd and Moscow ran fairly regularly. If one was fortunate enough to procure the necessary permission to travel, and a ticket, one could manage to make the journey without particular danger to life or limb. But the farther south one went the more apparent became the disorganization. Broken cars dotted the landscape, disabled engines lay along the route, and frequently the tracks were torn up. Everywhere in the Ukraina the stations were filled to suffocation, the people making a wild rush whenever a train was sighted. Most of them remained for weeks on the platforms before succeeding in getting into a train. The steps and even the roofs of the cars were crowded by men and women loaded with bundles and bags. At every station there was a savage scramble for a bit of space. Soldiers drove the passengers off the steps and the roofs, and often they had to resort to arms. Yet so desperate were the people and so determined to get to some place where there was hope of securing a little food, that they seemed indifferent to arrest and risked their lives continuously in this mode of travel. As a result of this situation there were numberless accidents, scores of travellers being often swept to their death by low bridges. These sights had become so common that practically no attention was paid to them. Travelling southward and on our return we frequently witnessed these scenes. Constantly the *meshotchniki* [people with bags] mobbed the cars in search of food, or when returning laden with their precious burden of flour and potatoes.

Day and night the terrible scenes kept repeating themselves at every station. It was becoming a torture to travel in our well-equipped car. It contained only six persons, leaving considerable room for more; yet we were forbidden to share it with others. It was not only because of the danger of infection or of insects but because the Museum effects and the material collected would have surely vanished had we allowed strangers on board. We sought to salve our conscience by permitting women and children or cripples to travel on the rear platform of our car, though even that was contrary to orders.

Another feature which caused us considerable annoyance was the inscription on our car, which read: Extraordinary Commission of the Museum of the Revolution. Our friends at the Museum had assured us that the "title" would help us to secure attention at the stations and would also be effective in getting our car attached to such trains as we needed. But already the first few days proved that the inscription roused popular feeling against us. The name "Extraordinary Commission" signified to the people the Tcheka. They paid no attention to the other words, being terrorized by the first. Early in the journey we noticed the sinister looks that met us at the stations and the unwillingness of the people to enter into friendly conversation. Presently it dawned on us what was wrong; but it required

considerable effort to explain the misunderstanding. Once put at his ease, the simple
Russian opened up his heart to us. A kind
word, a solicitous inquiry, a cigarette, changed his
attitude. Especially when assured that we were
not Communists and that we had come from
America, the people along the route would
soften and become more talkative, sometimes
even confidential. They were unsophisticated
and primitive, often crude. But illiterate and
undeveloped as they were, these plain folk were
clear about their needs. They were unspoiled
and possessed of a deep faith in elementary
justice and equality. I was often moved almost
to tears by these Russian peasant men and
women clinging to the steps of the moving train,
every moment in danger of their lives, yet remaining good-humoured and indifferent to their
miserable condition. They would exchange
stories of their lives or sometimes break out in
the melodious, sad songs of the south. At the
stations, while the train waited for an engine,
the peasants would gather into groups, form a
large circle, and then someone would begin to
play the accordion, the bystanders accompanying
with song. It was strange to see these hungry
and ragged peasants, huge loads on their backs.

standing about entirely forgetful of their environment, pouring their hearts out in folk songs. A peculiar people, these Russians, saint and devil in one, manifesting the highest as well as the most brutal impulses, capable of almost anything except sustained effort. I have often wondered whether this lack did not to some extent explain the disorganization of the country and the tragic condition of the Revolution.

We reached Poltava in the morning. The city looked cheerful in the bright sunlight, the streets lined with trees, with little garden patches between them. Vegetables in great variety were growing on them, and it was refreshing to note that no fences were about and still the vegetables were safe, which would surely not have been the case in Petrograd or Moscow Apparently there was not so much hunger in this city as in the north.

Together with the Expedition Secretary I visited the government headquarters. Instead of the usual *Ispolkom* [Executive Committee of the Soviet] Poltava was ruled by a revolutionary committee known as the *Revkom*. This indicated that the Bolsheviki had not yet had time to organize a Soviet in the city. We succeeded in getting the chairman of the *Revkom* interested in the purpose of our journey and he promised to coöperate and to issue an order to the various departments that material be collected and prepared for us. Our gracious reception augured good returns.

In the Bureau for the Care of Mothers and Infants I met two very interesting women—one the daughter of the great Russian writer, Korolenko, the other the former chairman of the Save-the-Children Society. Learning of the purpose of my presence in Poltava the women offered their aid and invited me to visit their school and the near-by home of Korolenko.

The school was located in a small house set deep in a beautiful garden, the place hardly visible from the street. The reception room contained a rich collection of dolls of every variety. There were handsome Ukrainian lassies, competing in colourful dress and headgear with their beautiful sisters from the Caucasus· dashing Cossacks from the Don looked proudly at their less graceful brothers from the Volga. There were dolls of every description, representing local costumes of almost every part of Russia. The collection also contained various toys, the handwork of the villages, and beautiful designs of the *kustarny* manufacture, representing groups of children in Russian and Siberian peasant attire.

The ladies of the house related the story of the Save-the-Children Society. The organization in existence, for a number of years, was of very limited scope until the February Revolution. Then new elements, mainly of revolutionary type, joined the society. They strove to extend its work and to provide not only for the physical well-being of the children but also to educate them, teach them to love work and develop their appreciation of beauty. Toys and dolls, made chiefly of waste material, were exhibited and the proceeds applied to the needs of the children. After the October Revolution, when the Bolsheviki possessed themselves of Poltava, the society was repeatedly raided and some of the instructors arrested on suspicion that the institution was a counter-revolutionary nest. The small band which remained went on, however, with their efforts on behalf of the children. They succeeded in sending a delegation to Lunacharsky to appeal for permission to carry on their work. Lunacharsky proved sympathetic, issued the requested document, and even provided them with a letter to the local authorities, pointing out the importance of their labours.

But the society continued to be subjected to annoyance and discrimination. To avoid being charged with sabotage the women offered their services to the Poltava Department of Education. There they worked from nine in the morning till three in the afternoon, devoting their leisure time to their school. But the antagonism of the Communist authorities was not appeased: the society remained in disfavour.

The women pointed out that the Soviet Government pretended to stand for self-determination and yet every independent effort was being discredited and all initiative discouraged, if not entirely suppressed. Not even the Ukrainian Communists were permitted self-determination. The majority of the chiefs of the departments were Moscow appointees, and Ukraina was practically deprived of opportunity for independent action. A bitter struggle was going on between the Communist Party of Ukraina and the Central authorities in Moscow. The policy of the latter was to control every thing.

The women were devoted to the cause of the children and willing to suffer misunderstanding and even persecution for the sake of their interest in the welfare of their charges. Both had understanding for and sympathy with the Revolution, though they could not approve of the terroristic methods of the Bolsheviki. They were intelligent and cultured people and I felt their home an oasis in the desert of Communist thought and feeling. Before I left the ladies supplied me with a collection of the children's work and some exquisite colour drawings by Miss Korolenko, begging me to send the things to America as specimens of their labours. They were very eager to have the American people learn about their society and its efforts.

Subsequently I had the opportunity of meeting Korolenko who was still very feeble from his recent illness. He looked the patriarch, venerable and benign; he quickly warmed one's heart by his melodious voice and the fine face that lit up when he spoke of the people. He referred affectionately to America and his friends there. But the light faded out of his eyes and his voice quivered with grief as he spoke of the great tragedy of Russia and the suffering of the people.

"You want to know my views on the present situation and my attitude toward the Bolsheviki?" he asked. "It would take too long to tell you about it. I am writing to Lunacharsky a series of letters for which he had asked and which he promised to publish. The letters deal with this subject. Frankly speaking, I do not believe they will ever appear in print, but I shall send you a copy of the letters for the Museum as soon as they are complete. There will be six of them. I can give you two right now. Briefly, my opinion is summarized in a certain passage in one of these letters. I said there that if the gendarmes of the Tsar would have had the power not only to arrest but also to shoot us, the situation would have been like the present one. That is what is happening before my eyes every day. The Bolsheviki claim that such methods are inseparable from the Revolution. But I cannot agree with them that persecution and constant shooting will serve the interests of the people or of the Revolution. It was always my conception that revolution meant the highest expression of humanity and of justice. In Russia to-day both are absent. At a time when the fullest expression and coöperation of all intellectual and spiritual forces are necessary to reconstruct the country, a gag has been placed upon the whole people. To dare question the wisdom and efficacy of the so-called dictatorship of the proletariat or of the

Communist Party leaders is considered a crime. We lack the simplest requisites of the real essence of a social revolution, and yet we pretend to have placed ourselves at the head of a world revolution. Poor Russia will have to pay dearly for this experiment. It may even delay for a long time fundamental changes in other countries. The bourgeoisie will be able to defend its reactionary methods by pointing to what has happened in Russia."

With heavy heart I took leave of the famous writer, one of the last of the great literary men who had been the conscience and the spiritual voice of intellectual Russia. Again I felt him uttering the cry of that part of the Russian *intelligentsia* whose sympathies were entirely with the people and whose life and work were inspired only by the love of their country and the interest for its welfare.

In the evening I visited a relative of Korolenko, a very sympathetic old lady who was the chairman of the Poltava Political Red Cross. She told me much about things that Korolenko himself was too modest to mention. Old and feeble as he was, he was spending most of his time in the Tcheka, trying to save the lives of those innocently condemned to death. He frequently wrote letters of appeal to Lenin, Gorki, and Lunacharsky, begging them to intervene to prevent senseless executions. The present chairman of the Poltava Tcheka was a man relentless and cruel. His sole solution of difficult problems was shooting. The lady smiled sadly when I told her that the man had been very gracious to the members of our Expedition. "That was for show," she said, "we know him better. We have daily occasion to see his graciousness from this balcony. Here pass the victims taken to slaughter."

Poltava is famous as a manufacturing centre of peasant handicrafts. Beautiful linen, embroidery, laces, and basket work were among the products of the province's industry. I visited the Department of Social Economy, the *sovnarkhoz*, where I learned that those industries were practically suspended. Only a small collection remained in the Department. "We used to supply the whole world, even America, with our *kustarny* work," said the woman in charge, who had formerly been the head of the *Zemstvo*, which took special pride in fostering those peasant efforts. "Our needlework was known all over the country as among the finest specimens of art, but now it has all been destroyed. The peasants have lost their art impulse, they have become brutalized and corrupted." She was bemoaning the loss of peasant art as a mother does that of her child.

During our stay in Poltava we got in touch with representatives of various other social elements. The reaction of the Zionists toward the Bolshevik régime was particularly interesting. At first they refused to speak with us, evidently made very cautious by previous experience. It was also the presence of our secretary, a Gentile, that aroused their distrust. I arranged to meet some of the Zionists alone, and gradually they became more confidential. I had learned in Moscow, in connection with the arrest of the Zionists there, that the Bolsheviki were inclined to consider them counter-revolutionary. But I found the Poltava Zionists very simple orthodox Jews who certainly could not impress any one as conspirators or active enemies. They were passive, though bitter against the Bolshevik régime. It was claimed that the Bolsheviki made no pogroms and that they do not persecute the Jews, they said; but that was true only in a certain sense. There were two kinds of pogroms: the loud, violent ones, and the silent ones. Of the two the Zionists considered the former preferable.

even murdered; and then it is over. But the silent pogroms continued all the time. They consisted of constant discrimination, persecution, and hounding. The Bolsheviki had closed the Jewish hospitals and now sick Jews were forced to eat *treife* in the Gentile hospitals. The same applied to the Jewish children in the Bolshevik feeding houses. If a Jew and a Gentile happened to be arrested on the same charge, it was certain that the Gentile would go free while the Jew would be sent to prison and sometimes even shot. They were all the time exposed to insult and indignities, not to mention the fact that they were doomed to slow starvation, since all trade had been suppressed. The Jews in the Ukraina were suffering a continuous silent pogrom.

I felt that the Zionist criticism of the Bol shevik régime was inspired by a narrow religious and nationalistic attitude. They were Orthodox Jews, mostly tradesmen whom the Revolution had deprived of their sphere of activity. Nevertheless, their problem was real—the problem of the Jew suffocating in the atmosphere of active anti-Semitism. In Poltava the leading Communist and Bolshevik officials were Gentiles. Their dislike of the Jews was frank and open. Anti-Semitism throughout the Ukraine was more virulent than even in pre-revolutionary days.

After leaving Poltava we continued on our journey south, but we did not get farther than Fastov owing to the lack of engines. That town, once prosperous, was now impoverished and reduced to less than one third of its former population. Almost all activity was at a standstill. We found the market place, in the centre of the town, a most insignificant affair, consisting of a few stalls having small supplies of white flour, sugar, and butter. There were more women about than men, and I was especially struck by the strange expression in their eyes. They did not look you full in the face; they stared past you with a dumb, hunted animal expression. We told the women that we had heard many terrible pogroms had taken place in Fastov and we wished to get data on the subject to be sent to America to enlighten the people there on the condition of the Ukrainian Jews. As the news of our presence spread many women and children surrounded us, all much excited and each trying to tell her story of the horrors of Fastov. Fearful pogroms, they related, had taken place in that city, the most terrible of them by Denikin, in September, 1919. It lasted eight days, during which 4,000 persons were killed, while several thousand died as the result of wounds and shock. Seven thousand perished from hunger and exposure on the road to Kiev, while trying to escape the Denikin savages. The greater part of the city had been destroyed or burned; many of the older Jews were trapped in the synagogue and there murdered, while others had been driven to the public square where they were slaughtered. Not a woman, young or old, that had not been outraged, most of them in the very sight of their fathers, husbands, and brothers. The young girls, some of them mere children, had suffered repeated violation at the hands of the Denikin soldiers. I understood the dreadful look in the eyes of the women of Fastov.

Men and women besieged us with appeals to inform their relatives in America about their miserable condition. Almost everyone, it seemed, had some kin in that country. They crowded into our car in the evenings, bringing scores of letters to be forwarded to the States. Some of the messages bore no addresses, the simple folk thinking the name sufficient. Others had not heard from their American kindred during the years of war and revolution but still hoped that they were to be found somewhere across the ocean. It was touching to see the people's deep faith that their relatives in America would save them.

Every evening our car was filled with the unfortunates of Fastov. Among them was a particularly interesting visitor, a former attorney, who had repeatedly braved the pogrom makers and saved many Jewish lives. He had kept a diary of the pogroms and we spent a whole evening listening to the reading of his manuscript. It was a simple recital of facts and dates, terrible in its unadorned objectivity. It was the soul cry of a people continuously violated and tortured and living in daily fear of new indignities and outrages. Only one bright spot there was in the horrible picture: no pogroms had taken place under the Bolsheviki. The gratitude of the Fastov Jews was pathetic. They clung to the Communists as to a saving straw. It was encouraging to think that the Bolshevik régime was at least free from that worst of all Russian curses, pogroms against Jews.

CHAPTER XXI

KIEV

OWING to the many difficulties and delays the journey from Fastov to Kiev lasted six days and was a continuous nightmare. The railway situation was appalling. At every station scores of freight cars clogged the lines. Nor were they loaded with provisions to feed the starving cities; they were densely packed with human cargo among whom the sick were a large percentage. All along the route the waiting rooms and platforms were filled with crowds, bedraggled and dirty. Even more ghastly were the scenes at night. Everywhere masses of desperate people, shouting and struggling to gain a foothold on the train. They resembled the damned of Dante's Inferno, their faces ashen gray in the dim light, all frantically fighting for a place. Now and then an agonized cry would ring through the night and the already moving train would come to a halt: somebody had been thrown to his death under the wheels.

It was a relief to reach Kiev. We had expected to find the city almost in ruins, but we were pleasantly disappointed. When we left Petrograd the Soviet Press contained numerous stories of vandalism committed by Poles before evacuating Kiev. They had almost demolished the famous ancient cathedral in the city, the papers wrote, destroyed the water works and electric stations, and set fire to several parts of the city. Tchicherin and Lunacharsky issued passionate appeals to the cultured people of the world in protest against such barbarism. The crime of the Poles against Art was compared with that committed by the Germans in Rheims, whose celebrated cathedral had been injured by Prussian artillery. We were, therefore, much surprised to find Kiev in even better condition than Petrograd. In fact, the city had suffered very little, considering the numerous changes of government and the accompanying military operations. It is true that some bridges and railroad tracks had been blown up on the outskirts of the city, but Kiev itself was almost unharmed. People looked at us in amazement when we made inquiries about the condition of the cathedral: they had not heard the Moscow report.

Unlike our welcome in Kharkov and Poltava, Kiev proved a disappointment. The secretary of the *Ispolkom* was not very amiable and appeared not at all impressed by Zinoviev's signature on our credentials. Our secretary succeeded in seeing the chairman of the Executive Committee, but returned very discouraged: that high official was too impatient to listen to her representations. He was busy, he said, and could not be troubled. It was decided that I try my luck as an American, with the result that the chairman finally agreed to give us access to the available material.[1] It was a sad reflection on the irony of life. America was in league with world imperialism to starve and crush Russia. Yet it was sufficient to mention that one came from America to find the key to everything Russian. It was pathetic, and rather distasteful to make use of that key.

In Kiev antagonism to Communism was intense, even the local Bolsheviki being bitter against Moscow. It was out of the question for any one coming from "the centre" to secure their coöperation unless armed with State powers. The Government employees in Soviet institu tions took no interest in anything save their rations. Bureaucratic indifference and incompetence in Ukraina were even worse than in Moscow and were augmented by nationalistic resentment against the "Russians." It was true also of Kharkov and Poltava, though in a lesser degree. Here the very atmosphere was charged with distrust and hatred of everything Muscovite. The deception practised on us by the chairman of the Educational Department of Kharkov was characteristic of the resentment almost every Ukrainian official felt toward Moscow. The chairman was a Ukrainian to the core, but he could not openly ignore our credentials signed by Zinoviev and Lunacharsky. He promised to aid our efforts but he disliked the idea of Petrograd "absorbing" the historic material of the Ukraina. In Kiev there was no attempt to mask the opposition to Moscow. One was made to feel it everywhere. But the moment the magic word "America" was spoken and the people made to understand that one was not a Communist, they became interested and courteous, even confidential. The Ukrainian Communists were also no exception.

The information and documents collected in Kiev were of the same character as the data gathered in former cities. The system of education, care of the sick, distribution of labour and so forth were similar to the general Bolshevik scheme. "We follow the Moscow plan," said a Ukrainian teacher, "with the only difference that in our schools the Ukrainian language is taught together with Russian." The people, and especially the children, looked better fed and clad than those of Russia proper: food was comparatively more plentiful and cheaper. There were show schools as in Petrograd and Moscow, and no one apparently realized the corrupting effect of such discrimination upon the teachers as well as the children. The latter looked with envy upon the pupils of the favoured schools and believed that they were only for Communist children, which in reality was not the case. The teachers, on the other hand, knowing how little attention was paid to ordinary schools, were negligent in their work. All tried to get a position in the show schools which were enjoying special and varied rations.

The chairman of the Board of Health was an alert and competent man, one of the few officials in Kiev who showed interest in the Expedition and its work. He devoted much time to explaining to us the methods of his organization and pointing out interesting places to visit and the material which could be collected for the

Museum. He especially called our attention to the Jewish hospital for crippled children.

I found the latter in charge of a cultivated and charming man, Dr. N——. For twenty years he had been head of the hospital and he took interest as well as pride in showing us about his institution and relating its history.

The hospital had formerly been one of the most famous in Russia, the pride of the local Jews who had built and maintained it. But within recent years its usefulness had become curtailed owing to the frequent changes of government. It had been exposed to persecution and repeated pogroms. Jewish patients critically ill were often forced out of their beds to make room for the favourites of this or that régime. The officers of the Denikin army were most brutal. They drove the Jewish patients out into the street, subjected them to indignities and abuse, and would have killed them had it not been for the intercession of the hospital staff who at the risk of their own lives protected the sick. It was only the fact that the majority of the staff were Gentiles that saved the hospital and its inmates. But the shock resulted in numerous deaths and many patients were left with shattered nerves.

The doctor also related to me the story of some of the patients, most of them victims of the Fastov pogroms. Among them were children between the ages of six and eight, gaunt and sickly looking, terror stamped on their faces. They had lost all their kin, in some cases the whole family having been killed before their eyes. These children often waked at night, the physician said, in fright at their horrible dreams. Everything possible was being done for them, but so far the unfortunate children had not been freed from the memory of their terrible experiences at Fastov. The doctor pointed out a group of young girls between the ages of fourteen and eighteen, the worst victims of the Denikin pogrom. All of them had been repeatedly outraged and were in a mutilated state when they came to the hospital; it would take years to restore them to health. The doctor emphasized the fact that no pogroms had taken place during the Bolshevik régime. It was a great relief to him and his staff to know that his patients were no longer in such danger. But the hospital had other difficulties. There was the constant interference by political Commissars and the daily struggle for supplies. "I spend most of my time in the various bureaus," he said, "instead of devoting myself to my patients. Ignorant officials are given power over the medical profession, continuously ha rassing the doctors in their work." The doctor himself had been repeatedly arrested for sabotage because of his inability to comply with the numerous decrees and orders, frequently mutually contradictory. It was the result of a system in which political usefulness rather than professional merit played the main rôle. It often happened that a first-class physician of well-known repute and long experience would be suddenly ordered to some distant part to place a Communist doctor in his position. Under such conditions the best efforts were paralysed. Moreover, there was the general suspicion of the *intelligentsia*, which was a demoralizing factor. It was true that many of that class had sabotaged, but there were also those who did heroic and self-sacrificing work. The Bolsheviki, by their indiscriminate antagonism toward the *intelligentsia* as a class, roused prejudices and passions which poisoned the mainsprings of the cultural life of the country. The Russian *intelligentsia* had with its very blood fertilized the soil of the Revolution, yet it was not given it to reap the fruits of its long struggle. "A tragic fate," the doctor remarked; "unless one forget it in his work, existence would be impossible."

The institution for crippled children proved a very model and modern hospital, located in the heart of a large park. It was devoted to the marred creatures with twisted limbs and deformed bodies, victims of the great war, disease, and famine. The children looked aged and withered; like Father Time, they had been born old. They lay in rows on clean white beds, baking in the warm sun of the Ukrainian summer. The head physician, who guided us through the institution, seemed much beloved by his little charges. They were eager and pleased to see him as he approached each helpless child and bent over affectionately to make some inquiries about its health. The hospital had been in existence for many years and was considered the first of its kind in Russia. Its equipment for the care of deformed and crippled children was among the most modern. "Since the war and the Revolution we feel rather behind the times," the doctor said; "we have been cut off from the civilized world for so

strife and disease." The supplies for the institution were provided by the Government and the hospital force was exposed to no interference, though I understood from the doctor that because of his political neutrality he was looked upon by the Bolsheviki as inclined to counter-revolution.

The hospital contained a large number of children; some of those who could walk about studied music and art, and we had the opportunity of attending an informal concert arranged by the children and their teachers in our honour. Some of them played the *balalaika* in a most artistic manner, and it was consoling to see those marred children finding forgetfulness in the rhythm of the folk melodies of the Ukraina.

Early during our stay in Kiev we learned that the most valuable material for the Museum was not to be found in the Soviet institutions, but that it was in the possession of other political groups and private persons. The best statistical information on pogroms, for instance, was in the hands of a former Minister of the Rada régime in the Ukraina. I succeeded in locating the man and great was my surprise when, upon learning my identity, he presented me with several copies of the *Mother Earth* magazine I had published in America. The ex-Minister arranged a small gathering to which were invited some writers and poets and men active in the Jewish *Kulturliga* to meet several members of our Expedition. The gathering consisted of the best elements of the local Jewish *intelligentsia*. We discussed the Revolution, the Bolshevik methods, and the Jewish problem. Most of those present, though opposed to the Communist theories, were in favour of the Soviet Government. They felt that the Bolsheviki, in spite of their many blunders, were striving to further the interests of Russia and the Revolution. At any rate, under the Communist régime the Jews were not exposed to the pogroms practised upon them by all the other régimes of Ukraina. Those Jewish intellectuals argued that the Bolsheviki at least permitted the Jews to live, and that they were therefore to be preferred to any other governments and should be supported by the Jews. They were fearful of the growth of anti-Semitism in Russia and were horrified at the possibility of the Bolsheviki being overthrown. Wholesale slaughter of the Jews would undoubtedly follow, they believed.

Some of the younger set held a different view.

The Bolshevik régime had resulted in increased hatred toward the Jews, they said, for the masses were under the impression that most of the Communists were Jews. Communism stood for forcible tax-collection, punitive expeditions, and the Tcheka. Popular opposition to the Communists therefore expressed itself in the hatred of the whole Jewish race. Thus Bolshevik tyranny had added fuel to the latent anti-Semitism of the Ukraina. Moreover, to prove that they were not discriminating in favour of the Jews, the Bolsheviki had gone to the other extreme and frequently arrested and punished Jews for things that the Gentiles could do with impunity. The Bolsheviki also fostered and endowed cultural work in the south in the Ukrainian language, while at the same time they discouraged such efforts in the Jewish language. It was true that the *Kulturliga* was still permitted to exist, but its work was hampered at every step. In short, the Bolsheviki permitted the Jews to live, but only in a physical sense. Culturally, they were condemned to death. The *Yevkom* (Jewish Communist Section) was receiving, of course, every advantage and support from the Government, but then its mission was to carry the gospel of the proletarian dictatorship to the Jews of the Ukraina. It was significant that the *Yevkom* was more anti-Semitic than the Ukrainians themselves. If it had the power it would pogrom every non-Communist Jewish organization and destroy all Jewish educational efforts. This young element emphasized that they did not favour the overthrow of the Bolshevik Government; but they could not support it, either.

I felt that both Jewish factions took a purely nationalistic view of the Russian situation. I could well understand their personal attitude, the result of their own suffering and the persecution of the Jewish race. Still, my chief concern was the Revolution and its effects upon Russia *as a whole* Whether the Bolsheviki should be supported or not could not depend merely on their attitude to the Jews and the Jewish question. The latter was surely a very vital and pressing issue, especially in the Ukraina; yet the general problem involved was much greater. It embraced the complete economic and social emancipation of the whole people of Russia, the Jews included. If the Bolshevik methods and practices were not imposed upon them by the force of circumstances, if they were conditioned in their own theories and principles, and if their sole object was to secure their **own power,** I could not support them. They might be innocent of pogroms against the Jews, but if they were pogroming the whole of Russia then they had failed in their mission as a revolutionary party. I was not prepared to say that I had reached a clear understanding of all the problems involved, but my experience so far led me to think that it was the basic Bolshevik conception of the Revolution which was false, its practical application necessarily resulting in the great Russian catastrophe of which the Jewish tragedy was but a minor part.

My host and his friends could not agree with my viewpoint: we represented opposite camps. But the gathering was nevertheless intensely interesting and it was arranged that we meet again before our departure from the city.

Returning to our car one day I saw a detachment of Red Army soldiers at the railway station. On inquiry I found that foreign delegates were expected from Moscow and that the soldiers had been ordered out to participate in a demonstration in their honour. Groups of the uniformed men stood about discussing the arrival of the mission. There were many expressions of dissatisfaction because the soldiers had been kept waiting so long. "These people come to Russia just to look us over," one of the Red Army men said; "do they know anything about us or are they interested in how we live? Not they. It's a holiday for them. They are dressed up and fed by the Government, but they never talk to us and all they see is how we march past. Here we have been lying around in the burning sun for hours while the delegates are probably being feasted at some other station. That's comradeship and equality for you!"

I had heard such sentiments voiced before, but it was surprising to hear them from soldiers. I thought of Angelica Balabanova, who was accompanying the Italian Mission, and I wondered what she would think if she knew how the men felt. It had probably never occurred to her that those "ignorant Russian peasants" in military uniform had looked through the sham of official demonstrations.

The following day we received an invitation from Balabanova to attend a banquet given in honour of the Italian delegates. Anxious to meet the foreign guests, several members of our Expedition accepted the invitation.

The affair took place in the former Chamber of Commerce building, profusely decorated for the occasion. In the main banquet hall long tables were heavily laden with fresh-cut flowers, several varieties of southern fruit, and wine. The sight reminded one of the feasts of the old bourgeoisie, and I could see that Angelica felt rather uncomfortable at the lavish display of silverware and wealth. The banquet opened with the usual toasts, the guests drinking to Lenin, Trotsky, the Red Army, and the Third International, the whole company rising as the revolutionary anthem was intoned after each toast, with the soldiers and officers standing at attention in good old military style.

Among the delegates were two young French Anarcho-syndicalists. They had heard of our presence in Kiev and had been looking for us all day without being able to locate us. After the banquet they were immediately to leave for Petrograd, so that we had only a short time at our disposal. On our way to the station the delegates related that they had collected much material on the Revolution which they intended to publish in France. They had become convinced that all was not well with the Bolshevik régime: they had come to realize that the dictatorship of the proletariat was in the exclusive hands of the Communist Party, while the common worker was enslaved as much as ever. It was their intention, they said, to speak frankly about these matters to their comrades at home and to substantiate their attitude by the material in their possession. "Do you expect to get the documents out?" I asked La Petit, one of the delegates. "You don't mean that I might be prevented from taking out my own notes," he replied. "The Bolsheviki would not dare to go so far—not with foreign delegates, at any rate." He seemed so confident that I did not care to pursue the subject further. That night the delegates left Kiev and a short time afterward they departed from Russia. They were never seen alive again. Without making any comment upon their disappearance I merely want to mention that when I returned to Moscow several months later it was generally related that the two Anarcho-syndicalists, with several other men who had accompanied them, were overtaken by a storm somewhere off the coast of Finland, and were all drowned. There were rumours of foul play, though I am not inclined to credit the story, especially in view of the fact that together with the Anarcho-syndicalists also perished a Communist in good standing in Moscow. But their disappearance with all the documents

explained.

The rooms assigned to the members of our Expedition were located in a house within a *passage* leading off the Kreschatik, the main street of Kiev. It had formerly been the wealthy residential section of the city and its fine houses, though lately neglected, still looked imposing. The *passage* also contained a number of shops, ruins of former glory, which catered to the well-to-do of the neighbourhood. Those stores still had good supplies of vegetables, fruit, milk, and butter. They were owned mostly by old Jews whose energies could not be applied to any other usefulness—Orthodox Jews to whom the Revolution and the Bolsheviki were a *bête noire*, because that had "ruined all business." The little shops barely enabled their owners to exist; moreover, they were in constant danger of Tcheka raids, on which occasions the provisions would be expropriated. The appearance of those stores did not justify the belief that the Government would find it worth while raiding them. "Would not the Tcheka prefer to confiscate the goods of the big delicatessen and fruit stores on the Kreschatik?" I asked an old Jew storekeeper. "Not at all," he replied; "those taxes."

The morning following the banquet I went down to the little grocery store I used to do my shopping in. The place was closed, and I was surprised to find that not one of the small shops near by was open. Two days later I learned that the places had all been raided on the eve of the banquet in order to feast the foreign delegates. I promised myself never to attend another Bol shevik banquet.

Among the members of the *Kulturliga* I met a man who had lived in America, but for several years now was with his family in Kiev. His home proved one of the most hospitable during my stay in the south, and as he had many callers belonging to various social classes I was able to gather much information about the recent history of Ukraina. My host was not a Communist: though critical of the Bolshevik régime, he was by no means antagonistic. He used to say that the main fault of the Bolsheviki was their lack of psychological perception. He asserted that no government had ever such a great opportunity in the Ukraina as the Communists. The people had suffered so much from the various occupations and were so op-

pressed by every new régime that they rejoiced
when the Bolsheviki entered Kiev. Everybody
hoped that they would bring relief. But the
Communists quickly destroyed all illusions.
Within a few months they proved themselves
entirely incapable of administering the affairs of
the city; their methods antagonized the people,
and the terrorism of the Tcheka turned even the
friends of the Communists to bitter enmity.
Nobody objected to the nationalization of industry and it was of course expected that the
Bolsheviki would expropriate. But when the
bourgeoisie had been relieved of its possessions
it was found that only the raiders benefited.
Neither the people at large nor even the proletarian class gained anything. Precious jewellery,
silverware, furs, practically the whole wealth
of Kiev seemed to disappear and was no more
heard of. Later members of the Tcheka strutted
about the streets with their women gowned in
the finery of the bourgeoisie. When private
business places were closed, the doors were locked
and sealed and guards placed there. But within
a few weeks the stores were found empty. This
kind of "management" and the numerous new
laws and edicts, often mutually conflicting,
served the Tcheka as a pretext to terrorize and

mulct the citizens and aroused general hatred against the Bolsheviki. The people had turned against Petlura, Denikin, and the Poles. They welcomed the Bolsheviki with open arms. But the last disappointed them as the first.

"Now we have gotten used to the situation," my host said, "we just drift and manage as best we can." But he thought it a pity that the Bolsheviki lost such a great chance. They were unable to hold the confidence of the people and to direct that confidence into constructive channels. Not only had the Bolsheviki failed to operate the big industries: they also destroyed the small *kustarnaya* work. There had been thousands of artisans in the province of Kiev, for instance; most of them had worked by themselves, without exploiting any one. They were independent producers who supplied a certain need of the community. The Bolsheviki in their reckless scheme of nationalization suspended those efforts without being able to replace them by aught else. They had nothing to give either to the workers or to the peasants. The city proletariat faced the alternative of starving in the city or going back to the country. They preferred the latter, of course. Those who could not get to the country engaged in trade, buying and selling jewellery, for instance. Practically everybody in Russia had become a tradesman, the Bolshevik Government no less than private speculators. "You have no idea of the amount of illicit business carried on by officials in Soviet institutions," my host informed me; "nor is the army free from it. My nephew, a Red Army officer, a Communist, has just returned from the Polish front. He can tell you about these practices in the army."

I was particularly eager to talk to the young officer. In my travels I had met many soldiers, and I found that most of them had retained the old slave psychology and bowed absolutely to military discipline. Some, however, were very wide awake and could see clearly what was happening about them. A certain small element in the Red Army was entirely transformed by the Revolution. It was proof of the gestation of new life and new forms which set Russia apart from the rest of the world, notwithstanding Bolshevik tyranny and oppression. For that element the Revolution had a deep significance. They saw in it something vital which even the daily decrees could not compress within the narrow Communist mould. It was their attitude

Communist State growing at the cost of the Revolution, and some of them even went so far as to voice the opinion that the Bolsheviki had become the enemies of the Revolution. But they all felt that for the time being they could do nothing. They were determined to dispose of the foreign enemies first. "Then," they would say, "we will face the enemy at home."

The Red Army officer proved a fine-looking young fellow very deeply in earnest. At first he was disinclined to talk, but in the course of the evening he grew less embarrassed and expressed his feelings freely. He had found much corruption at the front, he said. But it was even worse at the base of supplies where he had done duty for some time. The men at the front were practically without clothes or shoes. The food was insufficient and the Army was ravaged by typhoid and cholera. Yet the spirit of the men was wonderful. They fought bravely, enthusiastically, because they believed in their ideal of a free Russia. But while they were fighting and dying for the great cause, the higher officers, the so-called *tovaristchi*, sat in safe retreat and there drank and gambled and got rich by speculation. The supplies so desperately needed at the front were being sold at fabulous prices to speculators.

The young officer had become so disheartened by the situation, he had thought of committing suicide. But now he was determined to return to the front. "I shall go back and tell my comrades what I have seen," he said; "our real work will begin when we have defeated foreign invasion. Then we shall go after those who are trading away the Revolution."

I felt there was no cause to despair so long as Russia possessed such spirits.

I returned to my room to find our secretary waiting to report the valuable find she had made. It consisted of rich Denikin material stacked in the city library and apparently forgotten by everybody. The librarian, a zealous Ukrainian nationalist, refused to permit the "Russian" Museum to take the material, though it was of no use to Kiev, literally buried in an obscure corner and exposed to danger and ruin. We decided to appeal to the Department of Education and to apply the "American amulet." It grew to be a standing joke among the members of the Expedition to resort to the "amulet" in difficult situations. Such matters were always referred to Alex-

It required considerable persuasion to interest the chairman in the matter. He persisted in refusing till I finally asked him: "Are you willing that it become known in America that you prefer to have valuable historical material rot away in Kiev rather than give it to the Petrograd Museum, which is sure to become a world centre for the study of the Russian Revolution and where Ukraına is to have such an important part?" At last the chairman issued the required order and our Expedition took possession of the material, to the great elation of our secretary, to whom the Museum represented the most important interest in life.

In the afternoon of the same day I was visited by a woman Anarchist who was accompanied by a young peasant girl, confidentially introduced as the wife of Makhno. My heart stood still for a moment: the presence of that girl in Kiev meant certain death were she discovered by the Bolsheviki. It also involved grave danger to my landlord and his family, for in Communist Russia harbouring—even if unwittingly—a member of the Makhno *povstantsi* often incurred the worst consequences. I expressed surprise at the young woman's recklessness in thus walking into the very jaws of the enemy.

But she explained that Makhno was determined to reach us; he would trust no one else with the message, and therefore she had volunteered to come. It was evident that danger had lost all terror for her. "We have been living in constant peril for years," she said simply.

Divested of her disguise, she revealed much beauty. She was a woman of twenty-five, with a wealth of jet-black hair of striking lustre. "Nestor had hoped that you and Alexander Berkman would manage to come, but he waited in vain," she began. "Now he sent me to tell you about the struggle he is waging and he hopes that you will make his purpose known to the world outside." Late into the night she related the story of Makhno which tallied in all important features with that told us by the two Ukrainian visitors in Petrograd. She dwelt on the methods employed by the Bolsheviki to eliminate Makhno and the agreements they had repeatedly made with him, every one of which had been broken by the Communists the moment immediate danger from invaders was over. She spoke of the savage persecution of the members of the Makhno army and of the numerous attempts of the Bolsheviki to trap and kill Nestor. That failing, the Bolsheviki had murdered family, including her father and brother. She praised the revolutionary devotion, the heroism and endurance of the *povstantsi* in the face of the greatest difficulties, and she entertained us with the legends the peasants had woven about the personality of Makhno. Thus, for instance, there grew up among the country folk the belief that Makhno was invulnerable because he had never been wounded during all the years of warfare, in spite of his practice of always personally leading every charge.

She was a good conversationalist, and her tragic story was relieved by bright touches of humour. She told many anecdotes about the exploits of Makhno. Once he had caused a wedding to be celebrated in a village occupied by the enemy. It was a gala affair, everybody attending. While the people were making merry on the market place and the soldiers were succumbing to the temptation of drink, Makhno's men surrounded the village and easily routed the superior forces stationed there. Having taken a town it was always Makhno's practice to compel the rich peasants, the *kulaki*, to give up their surplus wealth, which was then divided among the poor, Makhno keeping a share for his army. Then he would call a meeting of the villagers, address them on the purposes of the *povstantsi* movement, and distribute his literature.

Late into the night the young woman related the story of Makhno and *makhnovstchina*. Her voice, held low because of the danger of the situation, was rich and mellow, her eyes shone with the intensity of emotion. "Nestor wants you to tell the comrades of America and Europe," she concluded, "that he is one of them—an Anarchist whose aim is to defend the Revolution against all enemies. He is trying to direct the innate rebellious spirit of the Ukrainian peasant into organized Anarchist channels. He feels that he cannot accomplish it himself without the aid of the Anarchists of Russia. He himself is entirely occupied with military matters, and he has therefore invited his comrades throughout the country to take charge of the educational work. His ultimate plan is to take possession of a small territory in Ukraina and there establish a free commune. Meanwhile, he is determined to fight every reactionary force."

Makhno was very anxious to confer personally with Alexander Berkman and myself, and he proposed the following plan. He would arrange

lence, the place being captured by surprise. The stratagem would have the appearance of our having been taken prisoners, and protection would be guaranteed to the other members of the Expedition. After our conference we would be given safe conduct to our car. It would at the same time insure us against the Bolsheviki, for the whole scheme would be carried out in military manner, similar to a regular Makhno raid. The plan promised a very interesting adventure and we were anxious for an opportunity to meet Makhno personally. Yet we could not expose the other members of the Expedition to the risk involved in such an undertaking. We decided not to avail ourselves of the offer, hoping that another occasion might present itself to meet the *povstantsi* leader.

Makhno's wife had been a country school teacher; she possessed considerable information and was intensely interested in all cultural prob lems. She plied me with questions about American women, whether they had really become emancipated and enjoyed equal rights. The young woman had been with Makhno and his army for several years, but she could not reconcile herself to the primitive attitude of her people in regard to woman. The Ukrainian woman, she said, was considered an object of sex and motherhood only. Nestor himself was no exception in this matter. Was it different in America? Did the American woman believe in free motherhood and was she familiar with the subject of birth control?

It was astonishing to hear such questions from a peasant girl. I thought it most remarkable that a woman born and reared so far from the scene of woman's struggle for emancipation should yet be so alive to its problems. I spoke to the girl of the activities of the advanced women of America, of their achievements and of the work yet to be done for woman's emancipation. I mentioned some of the literature dealing with these subjects. She listened eagerly. "I must get hold of something to help our peasant women. They are just beasts of burden," she said.

Early the next morning we saw her safely out of the house. The same day, while visiting the Anarchist club, I witnessed a peculiar sight. The club had recently been reopened after having been raided by the Tcheka. The local

Anarchists met in the club rooms for study and
lectures; Anarchist literature was also to be had
there. While conversing with some friends I
noticed a group of prisoners passing on the street
below. Just as they neared the Anarchist headquarters several of them looked up, having evidently noticed the large sign over the club
rooms. Suddenly they straightened up, took
off their caps, bowed, and then passed on. I
turned to my friends. "Those peasants are
probably *makhnovstsi*," they said; "the Anarchist
headquarters are sacred precincts to them."
How exceptional the Russian soul, I thought,
wondering whether a group of American workers or farmers could be so imbued with an
ideal as to express it in the simple and significant
way the *makhnovstsi* did. To the Russian his
belief is indeed an inspiration.

Our stay in Kiev was rich in varied experiences
and impressions. It was a strenuous time during which we met people of different social strata
and gathered much valuable information and
material. We closed our visit with a short trip
on the river Dniepr to view some of the old
monasteries and cathedrals, among them the
celebrated Sophievski and Vladimir. Imposing
edifices, which remained intact during all the

revolutionary changes, even their inner life continuing as before. In one of the monasteries we enjoyed the hospitality of the sisters who treated us to real Russian tea, black bread, and honey. They lived as if nothing had happened in Russia since 1914; it was as if they had passed the last years outside of the world. The monks still continued to show to the curious the sacred caves of the Vladimir Cathedral and the places where the saints had been walled in, their ossified bodies now on exhibition. Visitors were daily taken through the vaults, the accompanying priests pointing out the cells of the celebrated martyrs and reciting the biographies of the most important of the holy family. Some of the stories related were wonderful beyond all human credence, breathing holy superstition with every pore. The Red Army soldiers in our group looked rather dubious at the fantastic tales of the priests. Evidently the Revolution had influenced their religious spirit and developed a sceptical attitude toward miracle workers.

THE END

- Communist
- ✓ Proletariat
- ✗ ~~Plate~~ Bolshevik
- Anarchist
- ✓ Soviet

① SOVIET → Council, assembly, advice, harmony
    Council → political organizations
  and government bodies primarily associated
  with the Russian Revolution

② ~~Proletariat~~ → USSR (CCCP) →
  a socialist state uniting multiple subnational
  ~~Soviet~~ Soviet republics. one party →
  Communist Party

③ Bolsheviks → one of the majority. split apart
  from the Mensheviks (one of the minority)
  a major organization consisting primarily of workers

The beliefs are predecessors often referred to
as Bolshevism.   Founded by Lennen History of 1903
1917

③ Proletariat → workers or working-class
people → do not possess Capitalist
property

④ Bolshevism → Doctrine or program of
the Bolsheviks advocating violent overthrow
of Capitalism → Strategy developed by
the Bolsheviks between 1903 and 1917 with a
view to →p waging class warfare and establishment
a dictatorship of the proletariat.

CPSIA information can be obtained
at www.ICGtesting.com
Printed in the USA
LVOW13s0142011216
515251LV00030B/514/P